Diary of a
BAD Girl
Kingdom Style

IDELLA LISELLE

Scripture quotations taken from the Amplified® Bible,
Copyright © 1954, 1958, 1962, 1964, 1965, 1987 by The Lockman Foundation Used by permission." (**www.Lockman.org**)

Scripture quotations from *THE MESSAGE*. Copyright © by Eugene H. Peterson 1993, 1994, 1995, 1996, 2000, 2001, 2002. Used by permission of NavPress Publishing Group."

Scripture quotations marked "ESV" are taken from The Holy Bible: English Standard Version, copyright 2001, Wheaton: Good News Publishers. Used by permission. All rights reserved.

Scripture quotations marked "KJV" are taken from the Holy Bible, King James Version, Cambridge, 1769.

"Scripture quotations taken from the New American Standard Bible® (NASB), Copyright © 1960, 1962, 1963, 1968, 1971, 1972, 1973,1975, 1977, 1995 by The Lockman Foundation Used by permission. www.Lockman.org"

International Standard Book Number 13: 978-1948731003
Cover Design by Dream Design Graphics

Editing provided by Publishher Publishing

www.publishher.org

DEDICATION

This book is for BAD Girls all over the world.
What the enemy means for bad,
GOD will use for good.
And remember, it's okay to be BAD
(Bold, Anointed, & Dangerous)
as long as it's on PURPOSE

KINGDOM B.A.D GIRLS

BOLD, ANOINTED, & DANGEROUS

Kingdom BAD Girls are Bold, Anointed, & Dangerous.

- They don't need validation because, just like the Proverbs Women, they know their merchandise is good.
- They don't compete because they understand the world is a big enough stage to display and celebrate each and every one of our unique and diverse talents.
- They don't use their mouth to tear down because they understand their words carry the seeds of production, so they use it wisely.
- They are focused on endeavors that are fruitful and bring multiplication.
- They are intentional and unconventional.
- They use their differences as leverage, not limitations.
- They understand that they are created BAD on Purpose.

JOIN THE MOVEMENT

WWW.KINGDOMBADGIRLS.COM

CONTENTS

1

BAD ON PURPOSE
IDELLA LISELLE

But as for you, you meant evil against me; but GOD meant it for good, in order to bring it about as it is this day, to save many people alive. Genesis 50:20

Have you ever felt like life had it in for you? I mean, even from birth, you felt like the odds were always stacked against you. These thoughts almost breed a sense of helplessness. The next thing we know is that we are living a life braced for impact, always expecting the other shoe to drop.

To add salt to injury, a lack of a healthy foundation in early childhood allows for endless questioning of self- worth, value, and purpose.

Those on the outside would think that it was a setup for failure, but through more discerning eyes, one can see a masterful plan set in play, favored to have some interesting challenges in my life. At a young age, I knew there was something different about me. My dreams weren't the typical child's dreams.

While other children were dreaming of rainbows and lollipops, I was having dreams of fighting witches and warlocks. I was dreaming of saving drowning people or saving children, men, and women from buildings on the verge of collapsing.

I remember sharing some of those dreams in gory detail with my mother and her encouraging me that I had power even in my dreams. She told me to use the name of JESUS and that I was able to do anything in my dreams.

That piece of information was the game changer. No longer was I being tormented in my dreams. The fear was gone. Now, no matter what tried to appear, I knew I was powerful. I would fly in my dreams and walk on water in my dreams. Even as a child, I knew that there were some places where I could be unstoppable.

As for my dream space, I had that down, but my waking moments still had their bout of issues. At an early age, I was introduced to perversion. I was first shown how to touch myself at 7 by another little girl at a daycare. Then I saw my first pornographic magazine at the age of 9 with my brother and some neighborhood boys. At the age of 11, I was molested by a female family friend who had probably also been molested. The trap was set.

Since I first accepted JESUS CHRIST as my Savior at the age of 3, one would think all of the above could have been avoided. Right? Although my relationship with CHRIST grew, so did my struggles. A seed of perversion was planted, and through my insecurities, it grew. I so wanted to be accepted that I found myself in situations and scenarios that could have been avoided.

Again, I was saved at the age of 3, and most, if not ALL, of my sexual interactions happened within the confines of church activity and connections. I recall going to my friends twelfth birthday party at the age of 10. It took place at a hotel.

For those of us of a sound mind, it doesn't make sense for a twelve year old to have a hotel party with only GOD knowing exactly what's going on between the lewd dancing, groping, and what then was called "hunching" (one could consider this the equivalent to dry humping). However, since she was the pastor's daughter, it was okay, right?

As I rode back from the party, I remember a boy of twelve years pushing his hands between my legs to touch me and coming out with white fingers because the little ten-year-old girl had put powder on just like you do babies. I can laugh now, but then, it was no laughing matter.

I was in a highly sexual atmosphere among my church friends. I recall when the pastor's daughter pushed a boy on me and told us to "do it." I began screaming and saying, "No! I want to be a virgin until I am 11, 12, 13, 14, 15, 16...," and they pulled the guy off laughing. Though I was 10, many of my friends did not profess to be virgins. The pastor's daughter, at the age of 12, had already had several partners, some of whom were over 18.

It would appear that the odds were stacked against me, but GOD.

My need to be accepted swallowed my voice of resistance. I recall one occasion where the pastor's daughter who I looked up to made a request. She was very popular and had a lot of influence. So I complied. She asked me to take off my pants and lie on the floor. Feeling very uncomfortable, I still did. I then closed my eyes and prayed. Nothing happened, thank GOD. After seconds that seemed like hours, she laughed and told me to get up. She would share stories of how she would insert frozen hot dogs into her vagina. Seeds of perversion were being dropped, and ungodly desires grew.

Perversion was looking for me. At the age of 11, I was molested by an older female family friend. What should have been a safe place, was a place of strain and pressure. Seeking once again to be accepted, I allowed what I did not want. The light fondling always made me feel dirty. However, when she wanted to increase the intimacy, I found the courage to stand up and creatively removed myself from private encounters without confrontation.

The purpose of perversion goes to the root word, "pervert." "Pervert" means the alteration of something from its original course, meaning, or state to a distortion or corruption of what was first intended.

The enemy was trying to alter my course and distort my destiny. My over-exposure to sexual perversion had made me a secret freak. I was determined to keep the vow I made to CHRIST to be a virgin, but that was about it.

As a teenager, GOD had opened mighty doors of ministry. I was traveling with my youth group and promoting the gospel in unique ways and in uncommon settings. The more the doors opened, the greater the adversity.

The enemy wanted to steal my witness and stop my stride. I recall that there was a sister of a friend. She was about 1 or 2 years younger than me. One night we ended up with inappropriate touching. I remember feeling guilty after the interaction. I didn't coerce her, but is it possible that the same way I looked up to the pastor's daughter, she looked up to me?

We both went to church. My conviction had me to share with her that what we were doing was wrong and that we needed to repent, that included me asking her to forgive me for relating with her in that manner. She did, and we never did anything again

How did this happened I asked myself. The enemy was after my mind. He wanted me to *think* I was a lesbian.

I recall once when working as a director at a youth program, a young lady came to me and excitedly shared her new love interest. I listened as she giggled and shared who this person was. It was another young lady. I asked her when she began liking her. She replied it was after someone made the suggestion that they looked cute together and would make a good couple. That suggestion made her open to mentally entertain the idea.

She shared this hesitantly as if looking for my support. I first told her that regardless of her decision I would love her. Even though I may not be able to support her decision, I would always support her. Further conversation showed she didn't really like girls but was tired of guys doing her wrong. I shared that gender didn't remove the possibility of being cheated on or being done wrong. Integrity does. The same way a guy can dog you is the same way a girl can.

When asking if she ever thought about girls like that, she answered no, it wasn't until that comment did she even ever contemplate it. Think about today's pop culture and the many comments they are throwing our children's way. It is the subtlety of the enemy that we must pay close attention.

The mind is truly the gateway for all activity. Again the enemy wanted me to think I was a lesbian. I was able to quickly end those thoughts because I could never see myself kissing or desired to kiss a girl. And I loved kissing. Having a female partner held no appeal.

Perversion produces cycles, with or without our permission. To this day, I don't even know how my very short interaction began. It didn't make sense, I wasn't even attracted to girls, but perversion doesn't play fair and it desires to keep cycles going.

I left that encounter fully convinced that the alternate lifestyle was not for me. Since that situation was only a symptom and not the root, my battle with perversion wasn't over. The opposite was actually true - it was just beginning

Once you understand that perversion is wrapped in confusion, you stop trying to make sense of it in the natural and view it from the spiritual. Sexual perversion can't happen until spiritual perversion has already taken place. Though as a youth, I was being used more and more to minister on diverse stages, my relationship with GOD was apparently rocky. But I couldn't see that, remember perversion is the ultimate deception.

During this same time, I was also introduced to video pornography. One night, we had a girls night at a friend of my best friend's house. To my surprise, she brought out her parent's porn collection. Did I stop her? No! I didn't want to be labeled "the church girl," and there was a growing part of me that wanted to see what was on those tapes. Tape after tape, they played. The two girls shared the bed, they asked me if I desired to join them. I declined and chose the floor. I had no idea what they were doing up there because my focus was on my solo activity. Another door opened to perversion.

I remember seeing this boy in the neighborhood. He was tall, handsome, and lanky. When I inquired about him to a friend, she laughed as if I couldn't get him.

He had just graduated and apparently, in her opinion, was out of my league. Though I was only 15, I was already a senior and my friends were usually older than me. Therefore, his age wasn't a factor. Her comment made me determined to get him. We ended up getting together, and his experience mixed with my openness provided ample opportunity for sexual encounters.

In my opinion, I was still a Christian girl. I was still a virgin and guarding my virginity. I was skirting "the edge ministry," taking it as far as we can go but not doing "it." One night, he had sexually excited me to the point that I no longer cared about my virginity. Even with my sisters sleeping in the other room, I wanted it. His body was in upright agreement. I panted, "Let's do it." I know that it was not him who spoke in the following moment, but divine intervention. He said, "No. We can't, because you would hate me and yourself." I responded, "Excuse me? You have been begging me daily, but now no?" I was angry and asked him to leave. He later lied and said we did it. I laugh at how close his lie was to being true.

My mother taught us sex was a good thing. It was saved for marriage and that was for our protection. Therefore, the more we engaged in sexual activity, the more convicted I was. Yet I didn't stop. It was almost as if I couldn't stop, because I still wanted him and everything we did. It felt good. But we all know everything that feels good isn't always good for us.

Even as a youth, I wanted forever and I couldn't see me doing forever with him. He wasn't saved. I was able to disconnect from him after a few back-and-forths, but perversion was still there. At the end of the relationship, I actually repented to him for not being a witness of a true Christian girl. I knew that through all we did, my witness was shot. He looked surprised by the fact that I even repented but nodded in agreement.

I felt I had brought my interactions with men under subjection because I was trying to stay saved, but also a little of me was concerned that if I ever started having sex, I may not be able to stop. I was masking my issue but not uprooting it. You see, there was still a stronghold in place: masturbation and pornography.

One year, I became bold enough to share. I was about seventeen at an "I Kissed Dating Goodbye" meeting with Josh Harris. They had an altar call and I went up, and so followed my youth leader. I hesitantly shared with her my struggle with masturbation and what I was going through. She prayed with me, and that was it. There was no follow-up, no instructions, just a prayer.

So fast forward twelve years later. The struggle is still real. I would stand for a couple of months and then fall flat on my face. I recall the sense of shame because of my dirty little secret, yet my desperation for freedom was increasing. Desperation unleashes creativity.

I started putting out feelers. I was questioning whether I should share this with my pastor. At that time, his activities were becoming questionable. All of his close friends were VERY carnal. He would say that he liked real people. That piece of me that so wanted to be accepted didn't question such a statement. Who I am now would ask, "Why can't you find real people who are saved? They do exist, LOL."

My answer to whether I should share or not arrived one night when we were at my pastor's new girlfriend's house. The pastor I had looked up to for years asked an Elder of the church to share a funny story. Mind you, this was in the midst of mixed company in every sense. Not only were there men and women, but also Christians and non-Christians, including a woman whose salvation I was praying for. The elder's story explained how when he masturbated, his release would be so strong that he would black out. Did I get my answer or what?

I went back to the drawing board. As I looked within the church I attended, I became fully aware that their struggles wouldn't allow my deliverance and that I would have to look elsewhere for the power to get free. Have you ever looked for someone else to be the example that you needed when GOD was actually choosing you to be that very example?

One night, when I was about to fall into temptation again, HOLY SPIRIT spoke and said, "What if this is the last time I let you do this? What if I totally take my Spirit from you and you never hear from me again?"

I started crying. I couldn't imagine not hearing GOD's voice. As a child, I heard it so clearly that I ran into my parents' room and asked if they had called. I did it twice.

The second time, my mother said, "If you hear it again, say, 'LORD your servant hears you.'" Daily for years, my mother would have us get a Word of Knowledge from the LORD. She somehow incorporated an "Ask GOD" into every conversation. It was then that I understood the cry of David like never before - LORD, whatever You do, please don't take your presence away from me.

I immediately reached out to my mother who was also my spiritual mother. I shared my struggle. I reached out again and asked a local friend to be my accountability partner. I studied Scriptures on desires because it was my desire that was pulling me away. I fasted and I prayed. I removed myself from situations and environments that were contrary to my desire.

Needless to say, I had to remove myself from the leadership in my church of that time along with certain cliques. Know this, what leaders can't deal with in their lives, they won't be able to deal with in yours. I recall running out of my house one day to sit on the porch in order to make it impossible to fall. I did those types of things frequently until I had successfully crucified the flesh in that area.

In one interesting night after a couple of weeks of freedom, HOLY SPIRIT told me to share my testimony. I was like, "LORD, there are people here who don't know me, and more importantly, there are those who do."

I felt the impression of HOLY SPIRIT increase. I yielded and shared my testimony. Two of the women repented. One of the women who was the host said she was going to throw her dildo away.

As I saw what freedom not only did for me but through me for others, I was encouraged. I could see how that same sin that the enemy wanted to use to take me out would be the same sin that I would take on to be the voice crying in the wilderness that they could be free.

December 2004 was my date of victory. It is now almost 14 years since I claimed my freedom. But before you throw a parade and start the party, freedom is work! At any time, you can fall back.

Seven years ago, I was talking to a pastor. He obviously battled a spirit of lust. On one of our phone calls, he informed me that my voice stimulated him so that he pleasured himself. This should've been a red flare screaming "run!" But not for me. "I am the bishop of the Edge Ministry,".

I had a tendency of playing things close. The flirtations were back and forth. There was one instance where I was returning from a mission trip one day and going on a mission trip the next. I was in the pastor's city and decided to text him, "Hey I am in your city." That simple text evoked a sexual rant that was one for the records.

His words were a little tantalizing until he added profanity. From then on it was a complete turn off. I told him we couldn't do any of the things he suggested. I ended the texting and went to my Pastors and Bishop Meeting. The meeting was finished. I heard HOLY SPIRIT say, "Show your texts to the Apostle." "What?!" I thought, "I knew I should have deleted those texts." I obeyed and revealed the text messages. It seemed like it took him forever to read the text. He read them and told me that I was the one who started that. Who? Me? I didn't say anything.

Yet my heart had been opened to entertain it. He asked if I had repented, and I said I did. He jokingly said, "Be glad, daughter, because you would have been disappointed. A man with that much talk probably doesn't have a lot of action."

I was packing my bag, getting ready for the airport, when I heard HOLY SPIRIT say, "I am hurt that you would play with that." His pain brought me to my knees, and it was in that moment that I experienced godly sorrow. I was broken. It was then that I vowed to not just abstain from sex, but to be Holy.

Desiring holiness brought things into clear perspective because anything that has to be hidden can't be holy. "The Edge Ministry" was removed. I no longer skirted the dangerous lines of sin, but aimed for my motives and intents to be fully pleasing.

Our victories at times can make us more vulnerable to our defeats. I have years under my belt. I am good. I don't battle with thoughts and ideas like I used to. The desire to masturbate isn't there. But we are encouraged to be sober and vigilant because the enemy is on watch.

About five years ago, my watch wasn't as strong. I was under a lot of pressure. I had allowed things in my environment that previously were unacceptable. The enemy tried to come back with pornography. I wasn't looking for it; it found me. Yet I entertained it for a little too long. I notified my accountability team and added more reinforcements spiritually and naturally.

I'll never forget the day after I alerted the team to pray. I had a dream. The dream opened up to a beautiful, girly bedroom. It looked like a princess's room. I saw a monster come in. He was wolf-like, and he was searching for something. He looked in the drawers under the bed and left in a rage. As soon as the door closed, I heard, "and he found nothing." I knew HOLY SPIRIT was alerting me that the enemy wanted to be able to find pornography in play so he would have legal right to attack and to steal my power. I hadn't come this far to give up.

I had firsthand experience with the power of perversion. It used anything it could to stop me so that you wouldn't be reading this book right now, so you wouldn't know that freedom from ALL perversion is available.

It wasn't perversion's intention that the molestation that I experienced be used as a platform to bring healing to many. It wasn't prepared for the countless people who struggled with a same-sex attraction or appetite to get delivered and set free by choice because of my testimony and strategic prayers.

It didn't want me to understand its plots and ploys against us to use shame to silence mighty men and women of GOD so they never got free but lived with incomplete anointings and diluted ministry. It didn't want me to bring attention, awareness, and assistance. I can see the meme "It wasn't ready, LOL."

I understood why perversion wanted to take me out, but I can stand today and say, "But as for you, perversion, you meant evil against me; but God meant it for good, in order to bring it about as it is this day, to save many people alive."

While the enemy meant things for bad, GOD made me BAD on purpose.

POINTS TO PONDER

1. What is perverting your destiny?

2. What has swallowed your voice? What has kept you silent?

3. Are you frustratingly looking for something in someone else that GOD wants to develop in   you?

4. Have you experienced godly sorrow in the area of your sin?

POINTS TO PRACTICE

1. REMOVE THE SHAME, SHARE THE SECRET You are only as sick as your secret. Share your secret with someone you trust who can hold you accountable to greater. It may not be in your direct environment. Be open to look outside your comfort zone.

2. Take it One Day At A Time

    Understand any form of deliverance is self-maintained. Once you experience a struggle, the enemy always knows where you live. It is up to you to decide whether you will open the door and entertain it or not.

3. Be Ye Ready

    There will come a time when GOD is going to ask you to share your testimony. Take time to develop your testimony and know key points.
    Don't get stuck in a routine. Ensure that you are hearing from GOD because GOD can have you share it differently each time.

POINTS TO PRAY

1. Psalms 139:23-24

    Search me, O God, and know my heart;
    Try me, and know my anxieties;
    24 And see if there is any wicked way in me,
    And lead me in the way everlasting.

    Ask GOD to search your heart. Our hearts are wicked and deceitful. Much can hide in our hearts.

It is in prayer that these things are exposed so they can be FULLY dealt with.

2. Psalms 144:1

    Praise the LORD, who is my rock. He trains my hands for war and gives my fingers skill for battle.

    Hands can be symbolic to activity and actions - basically, what we do. Ask GOD to give you the strategies and skill so that activities of your life would equip you for battle and war, not the opposite.

Prayer:
Heavenly Father, Good, Good Daddy,
For some, it may be hard to call You that. Some have experienced horrible things at the hands of their fathers. Some don't know who their fathers are. Others don't have good relationships with their father. We now know and understand that this is a perversion of Your will and Your way.
In the absence of a natural father, I thank You that You will personally demonstrate the love of a Father, that in this very moment, You will wrap them in Your arms and love on them.
Love the shame off of them. I cancel every spirit of condemnation that would use the perversion to cause question to their value and their worth.
I thank You that in Your hands, even the most ugly thing can become something that is able to display the beauty of Your love. Someway, somehow, I am convinced that You in Your Sovereignty allow all things to work for our good. Wow, GOD, for our good. The first time we see good in Your word, it was pronounced only after something was doing what it was created to do.

We ask for your forgiveness for any participation with perversion, knowingly or unknowingly. LORD, we repent for allowing past perversions or any residue to stop us from pursuing and fulfilling our purpose.

We decree and declare that as we have confessed our sin, we are forgiven and renewed. We are Your workmanship. Even with the scars of life, LORD, through our obedience and participation, Your beauty is still able to shine through. Thank You that it is only through You that we are BAD on Purpose. In JESUS CHRIST'S name. Amen.

2
UNKNOWN VALUABLES
JULIE JONES

A jewel is defined as a precious gem, an ornament decorated, something worn as an accessory, one that is highly esteemed. Gems are formed deep within the earth's mantle. They are hidden until there is a volcanic eruption or until they reach the surface through erosion. This chapter is not Geology 101; rather, it's about the discovery of what is hidden, who you are through some eruptions and erosions that have brought you to the surface.

Growing up, my father would gift me jewelry such as rings, bracelets, and necklaces that had amethysts in them. They were beautiful, and not only that, but they were gifts that my father would give me on birthdays and other special occasions. I made sure that I kept the box and protected it in order to keep the jewelry from being lost. As careful as I was with keeping my jewelry safe, I didn't always do the same for myself.

My esteem was fashioned and formed from the words of others, or lack of words, not always words that made you feel good at times. I learned early on that pleasing people made others feel good, and that made me feel good.

The ability to say no to a request was not in my vocabulary. The moment I was called on to help or was needed, I jumped on the opportunity. For some, I wanted to help, and for others, I didn't. Yet I did anyway because I didn't want people to be mad at me. I cared so much about what others thought of me because this was what fed me. There is a saying we have heard, "you are what you eat," and scripture teaches us that as a man thinks, so is he.

Walking the halls of middle and high school from one class to the next, I welcomed the whispers, winks, and words that would come my way. I would walk by and say, "whatever" or give a look that indicated I didn't care, but in reality, it boosted my esteem whereas other girls would respond with an immediate punch or a verbal exchange to let that boy know, "next time, don't even think about it." Finding my voice was and continues to be a journey.

Turning 13 is a pivotal point for an adolescent. I was a teenager, and with that, I expected independence and believed that I could handle anything that came my way. I had met a peer from a neighboring school through a mutual friend. We all met up one night at a house and had a little drink. This made me feel mature and grown. One of my girlfriends "hooked up" with another mutual guy friend while the rest of us listened and hung out downstairs. I felt a bit uncomfortable. It was one of those I-have-a-friend-and-you-have-a-friend-so-we'll-hook- them-up situations. As I sat there with a young man, we kissed. One kiss had led to another opportunity. He had asked me to meet him there. I was excited by the invitation and I somehow managed to get there. He led me upstairs through this cold and dark house and into one of the bedrooms. I knew of him. He was popular, and I thought I must be somebody or worthy because he called me and wanted to spend time with me. I equated physical touch with worthiness. I equated sex with love. I trusted him. I felt special and scared at the same time. This was my first time.

I had found myself hooked on someone who didn't feel the same towards me. We would see each other at sports events and school activities, but he would ignore me, and I accepted it to be so. Then later on that night, I would get a phone call, no apology or explanation needed. The title, "friends with benefits," was enough for me. It was better than nothing. Going forward, this is how it would be for the next couple of years. I would withdraw plans at the drop of a dime if he wanted to meet or go somewhere. I snuck out in the middle of the night. I gave him money. I settled for sex and was ok with it. I was a buried gem, and I didn't even know it. It was hidden. There had soon come a turn of events in this relationship. It had come to my attention that there was a video of us that had been shown. I was confused. I didn't know who to believe, those who told me what to believe or the one who claimed he didn't do it and that he knew nothing of what was said. I was about 15, and we stopped talking. It was then that someone very close to me said, "Nobody will ever want to be with you now." Those words shaped me and every action following. They also put a wedge in my relationship with the person who spoke them.

You might be wondering what or where my relationship with God was. I grew up Catholic. I didn't have any intimate relationship with God, although, at the time, I thought making sacraments qualified. Ultimately, these were celebrations in which I received money. Going to church was a chore, and the only part I liked of it was homily.

This was the part where the priest would make a connection from the Gospel to current day life. Jesus describes it best when He addresses the Pharisees and discusses how the outside of the cup is clean but the inside is dirty, or when He instructs the disciples to follow the Pharisees words rather than their actions because they did not practice what they preached. Going to church was my connection to Jesus. When I would sin, I would just go to confession and my sins were forgiven because of the prayers I prayed. There was no mention about the gift of salvation to help me understand the blood of Jesus. It wasn't just my confirmation that I was making, if you know what I mean.

For the years following, I would entertain the advances or attention from guys, and without considering my safety or security, I would go along with it. If the guy pursued me and I thought he was attractive, then I would engage. I didn't consider myself promiscuous. I wasn't one of "those girls," and it wasn't as if I had multiple partners at the same time. With each encounter, whether it was with the same person or another individual, there was hope that it might turn into something more, but I would give so much of myself looking for a return to the point that there was nothing left of me.

Remember, I shared that I just couldn't say no. I would be hurt and not able to say no. These engagements had rules that were usually unspoken, yet people were aware that to expect anything more was ludicrous. I deserved better, I thought; however, I didn't really think that at the time because when your mind is set to settle or believes that only this exists, you will settle. I had no standard for myself. I was conformed to a pattern that had only led me to what I already knew what would come next: unhealthy and risky behavior in the name of love, a feel-good moment, validation.

I was like a robot, programmed to a pattern of inputs and outputs and expecting something different. I waited for something to change. I, too, was like the man at the pool of Bethesda lying on the bed, and I also felt pimped out like the concubine in Judges 19. The only thing different was that I threw myself out there. There were moments when I settled to be the "side chick." I would return to past relationships (vomit) and endure whatever because they called out to me, so I would be there. That, too, came with a pattern.

Usually, they would call with an issue or some line to reel me in, and I would take the bait. I didn't recognize it at the time, but there were cycles of these patterns. As long as the enemy can keep you within the cycle of a pattern, it keeps you from reaching and walking in divine purpose and destiny. Knowing your identity is crucial to breaking the vicious and repetitious cycles in one's life.

I wanted to be made whole. Therefore, I needed to follow the instructions that Jesus gave to the man at the pool of Bethesda, to pick up my bed and walk.

I was casting my pearls before swine because I didn't know my identity, my worth, my value. In fact, I didn't believe I had pearls, but pebbles. This was a struggle because I wanted others to value me. Instead, they would pick up, kick, or skip because that's what you do with pebbles and not pearls.

Sex is not love. Sex is a product of love, and sex without love is lust. I was in a relationship with lust. What looked good, sounded good, or smelled good, I wanted and accepted. Perversion produces lust and not purity. My concept of worth and value was perverted. What lie have you believed that has perverted your perspective? I'll let you know that truth will uncover every lie. Truth is needed to demolish every lie that you believe.

Growing up, my earthly father would call me a jewel. He would say, "you're not just a jewel by name but a jewel by nature." It sounded nice, and I felt special at the time, but its effect did not last. I didn't feel like a jewel. It wasn't until I was embraced by the love of God that He began to show me my value because I am HIS jewel.

The stronghold that had been erected and edified of people-pleasing, seeking value and worth through sexual encounters, bootie calls, and sneaking- peeking- lunch freaking, believing this is what I needed to do. As I grow in the knowledge of who God is through Jesus Christ, am transformed by the renewing of my mind, and am empowered by Holy Spirit, I am loving me because He loved me first. Love yourself enough to say no to certain invites without feeling guilty or that you're hurting someone's feelings.

I used to try and please people, even if that meant I was hurting myself as a result. However, I eventually began to trust the advice of Holy Spirit had I not it would've set me on another course of past patterns. He wants to plow a new path that is constructed and paved by His word. The power of God can do that.

I have been celibate now for 6 years since my divorce. While I know that sex before marriage is a sin, I didn't want to just be programmed by the word, but transformed, to know that God wants His bride without spot or blemish and to know what marriage is and why being made whole became my pursuit so that I would not fall prey to a carnal desire.

I began to appreciate the gentlemen that the Lord put in my path. I began respecting myself. I realized I didn't have male friends without the expectation of the relationship being sexual. These were healthy relationships of mutual respect and communication. This was a beautiful thing. God was healing wounds of rejection, filling me up with life, and allowing me to grow into the woman He called me to be, a witness for singles. Was it easy? No. Have I felt lonely? Yes.

As you stay in tune with Holy Spirit, you begin to be sensitive to various emotions and feelings. It is at this time you are vulnerable. It is in vulnerable times that you call on Him, and be honest because He knows our thoughts from afar off, and He knows the intents of our hearts. Set yourself around prayer warriors. Be aware that even in the areas where you have been delivered, you must continue to guard your heart and mind.

Here is an area of caution: there may be times where you encounter familiar people, places, and things that will bring a thought, a memory, or a replay to the surface. Remember that the Word instructs us to take every thought captive to the obedience of Christ. Consider when Jesus shared a point in the book of Matthew where He said not to commit adultery, but that if anyone was to look at a woman with lust in his heart, he has already committed adultery. We must be aware of the gates of our minds, eyes, ears, mouth, and nose and keep them guarded.

There are hidden jewels within us, jewels that will be discovered as we expose ourselves to the presence of God. Regardless of the volcanic activity from your past or your present, it does not compare to the glory that will be revealed in you. Creation is waiting eagerly for you to discover, develop, and deliver the jewel of a son or daughter that you are! You are precious, you are His accessory and an ornament of His love.

POINTS TO PONDER

1. You are a jewel! Zech 9:16. Receive and embrace God's unconditional love. He draws us to Himself with His loving kindness. And because of His love towards us, thus we are able to love. Love yourself and others.

2. Identify whose thoughts, what thoughts, and what words have shaped you. You were on the mind of God before He formed you in your mother's womb. You have been created in His own image. His thoughts toward you are for good thoughts to prosper you. How precious are HIS thoughts toward you! You are fearfully and wonderfully made!

3. Through the erosions and eruptions of life, what gems have you found within? It just might have taken these volcanic eruptions for you to see your purpose. It also

25

brings exposure to the issues within. For out of the abundance of the heart, the mouth speaks. God desires for you to be made whole! He desires truth in your inward parts! It's the knowledge of the truth that sets us free.

POINTS TO PRACTICE

1. Experience a deeper, intimate relationship with God by daily consumption of His Word and being in His presence. He promises in HIS Word that when we draw near to Him, He draws near to us. He longs to communicate with us. Spend time with Him. Relationships are strengthened through communication. We must develop a mindset of seeking. We are the apple of His eye. There are times when we become so busy that we remove God from first place in our lives. He is jealous for us!

2. Create a timeline to identify patterns and cycles that need to be broken. This is a great visual to see where and when we repeat cycles. This is an opportunity for deliverance and breakthrough to take place. God is ever ready for us to recognize and surrender to Him. It is through the blood of Christ Jesus that we have been set free. He is the WAY, TRUTH and the LIFE. We can experience the abundant life that He has laid out for us.

3. Speak words of life, love, and liberty over yourself. I am the righteousness of Christ. I can do all things through Christ Jesus who strengthens me. I am free to love me because Jesus loves me. My tongue has the power of life and death in it, and today I choose to speak life over myself and those connected to me.

POINTS TO PRAY

Heavenly Father, we give YOU thanks and praise! We adore YOU! I accept and believe that YOU have created me [your name] in YOUR image and likeness. I am valuable because I am YOURS. I am valuable because YOU have chosen me, a royal priesthood, a holy nation, a people for YOUR own possession, so that I may proclaim the excellencies of HIM who has called me out of darkness into YOUR marvelous light. YOU are the light of my salvation, YOU are love and YOU love me even in the depth of sin, even while lost, hurt, and confused. You are my savior, King, healer, deliverer, and redeemer! YOUR banner over me is LOVE!

3
STILL STANDING
JHAKI DAVIS

Here's the deal, all of my life there was a part of me that longed to be accepted by others without having to jump through hoops. Accept me for who I am, a human-being with strengths and weaknesses, good days and bad bays, who has likes and dislikes, but still somebody who is easy to get along with and hang with. I wanted to be received by others who also knew that I was growing and still trying to figure out who I am.

Being born in a military family afforded me wonderful opportunities. It had its advantages, which I am grateful for. Never would I want to trade the experience of living in different parts of the world, which comes with the territory.

However, one piece of this lifestyle I could have done without. New schools meant being the new kid on the block, and often, I had to fight to gain the status of acceptance on somebody else's turf. Other than kindergarten, I have always attended the public schools.

This was an entirely different world from the military base school, where on base we had unspoken code that we were familiar with: we may be newbies, but we are family.

Public schools were a very different community, so I had to be just as tough as the next person or become the target of unnecessary harassment.

Around the age of 21, I was saved and very active in the church. Yet there was still a wild side of me that sought adventure and even a little recklessness. Nothing I would call at the time "major" at the time. I only did it for kicks and an adrenaline rush. For instance, I would go to the beach and run as fast as I could and jump off a steep sloping hill. One time I unstrapped my seatbelt on a roller coaster ride. I did not like riding roller coasters back then, and still I don't like riding the, now. It was all for the rush.

On another occasion, at night, while there was no traffic on the road, I drove my car from one traffic light to the next traffic light, just to see if my car would get through the signal while it was still green. Looking back, I realize that this behavior was my way of dealing with depression and needing a way out. My recklessness was a cry for help, one of which seemed to go unnoticed by the people around me.

The same night as my speeding bravado, I had a dream that made me think twice about a lot of things. In this dream, I was somewhere, but at first, I couldn't see where. All I could see were people entering a church. I could hear them talking among themselves and some were crying.

I noticed a group of people who I recognized. The people were talking as they approached the front of the church. As they got closer, one lady who was shaking her head in disbelief, said, "This didn't have to happen. She was too young and had so much going for her." At that moment, I was looking up from a casket into the hurting eyes of people who expressed their care for me. I realized then that I was the reason for the gathering at the church. They were attending my funeral. It was too late for me to make some corrections for any of my inappropriate choices. When I saw that scene, I was scared straight. Isn't it ironic how even when we think we don't want to live, we truly don't want to die?

On another occasion, I remember riding in the back seat of my parents' vehicle, lying down and looking up in the dark of night. There was not a star in the sky. It was pitch black, and the moon was full and bright.

As I looked at the sky, I could hear these words spoken to me, "Though darkness be all around, I will be there." Wow! That was a powerful statement. I wanted to shoot straight up in my seat and ask my parents if they heard that, but decided not to. I knew that the LORD spoke to me. So, I just laid there and pondered the words over and over. At the time, I was not fully aware of the great magnitude that these words represented.

Years would pass. I got married and had a son. Things were going rather good, or so I thought. Situations arose that tested my tongue and my faith, but nothing that would push me to the edge of wanting to put it all on the line and walk away. I still felt I was okay; GOD and I, we got this. Somehow, another turn of events caused the rug to be snatched out from under me where everything appeared to spiral out of my control. My world turned upside down. I felt abandoned by all and mostly by GOD. My trust felt betrayed, and that's when the fight for my life really began.

GOD gave me another dream. In this dream, I had on a white robe and I was walking. I saw JESUS further ahead, and He told me to walk towards Him. As I stepped forward, various items were thrown at me, such as rocks, broken glass bottles, rotten fruit, etc. Some of the objects cut me, and I bled. When I turned to see who was throwing these things, I saw familiar faces, people I knew. They were hump-backed, large heads, raggedy clothes; and all were imperfect people throwing these harmful objects. My first reaction was to pick up a rock or two, or maybe a few bottles and retaliate, but I could hear JESUS say to me, "Stay focused and keep your eyes on me."

I replied, "Okay, but don't you see these people and what's going on here? Make them stop!" Yet, I was met with the same words, "Stay focused and keep your eyes on me." While all the hurtful objects kept coming, I turned, fixed my eyes on JESUS, did as He said and found myself in the outstretched arms of my Savior.

In the following weeks, that dream became a reality. Trust me when I say that things didn't get any better but became worse. Seemingly, every step of progress was met with obstacles that forced me several steps backwards. Getting past this kind of barricade felt impossible. It was opposition after opposition. At this point, my tolerance scale was beyond negative 10. My prayer was, "GOD, why? And don't tell me 'because'. I want an answer." One day, as soon as those words left my mouth, GOD answered softly, "Because, I didn't have anyone else who could, but you." The tons of weights I had once felt, became lighter as I felt the presence of the LORD come along side me and share the burden. The impossible became the possible. All what seemed like darkness surrounding me now felt like light encompassing me. That day was a turnaround for me. I could see clearer and had better understanding.

All four of these events, though occurred at different times in my life, are connected to each other. The first dream showed what would happen if the LORD had not intervened that day. Yes, reckless in my younger years and the pending behavior that day was rash; it could have resulted in death, and all the lives connected could have been changed forever.

I never once imagined that what I endured through elementary and middle school, could happen in the church, a safe haven that I attended, where the song "Just As I Am" was sung. Yep, the methods or actions were different, but the same behavior was still present. It was like being initiated into a sorority or fraternity. Let me tell you, for the most part, initiations can be grueling.

Once again, I was the new kid on the block, who was about to be casted into the lion's' den just to prove who I am or what I am made of. It was open season all over again. Though I tried to no avail, I could not do anything right.

Every action, re-action, and non-action was under scrutiny, and if it did not meet with the approval of others, somehow and some way, I paid for it. "GOD, I didn't sign up for this" was my cry. My "This too will pass" was nowhere in sight. The most frequently asked questions that I found coming out of my mouth were, "Where does it end?" and "I'm not perfect, don't these people have nothing else better to do?" Enough was enough.

Resentment, anger, hatred and bitterness were all pounding at the door of my heart. Each one had a foot across the threshold, trying to bombard their way in and I was leaning against the door, about to buckle because the pressure had become too forceful to resist. I felt rejected, betrayed, and unaccepted. It felt like whatever I had to offer or add was not appreciated. It appeared impossible to obtain approval. I had fallen into a pit and did not see a way out.

Nagging questions plagued my mind. Where do I turn? Who could help me? Could anyone see I'm in dire need? I felt there was no strength left in me to do this alone. Slipping into a deep depression became the way of escape. Because then, however the chips may fall, I no longer had to considered myself responsible. I felt as if the next push would take me to a place of no return. I wanted to give up, but GOD's love for me would not allow me to throw in the towel.

HE designed a test just for me. It was divinely orchestrated to lift me out the pit. The ordeal caused me to meet and wrestle with my issues, surrender my all and wholly pledge my true devotion to the Father. This commitment was not hinged on being a people pleaser, being in my feelings, and jumping through hoops to be liked.

My goal then became to be so in love with GOD that it didn't matter how others treat me or mistreat me. Most of us know that what matters at the end of the day, is how we respond and treat others.

Yes, some of my actions were self-inflicted. However, Praise be to GOD, in my foolishness, those actions did not take me out. Each time in my life when circumstances came at me hard and all seemed hopeless, I would take courage and rehearse those divine encounters and a verse from a song that says, "HE brought us to it, to bring us through." I really take hold of the Scripture that instructs me to "Be strong and courageous. Do not be afraid or terrified because of them, for the LORD your GOD goes with you; He will never leave you nor forsake you." (Deuteronomy 31:6 KJV). I rest in the fact, knowing without a shadow of doubt that He [GOD] really loves me and is for me.

There were times when all was dark around me, but I had to know that the LORD, was with me and I had to hold fast to that truth - truth which is a promise.

I would re-live that moment in the back seat, hear those very words spoken to me as if it was the first time. I would remember the dreams and words of encouragement and use all of that as an instrument to keep me going.

Philippians 1:6 (KJV) states, "Being confident of this very thing, that he which hath begun a good work in you will perform it until the day of Jesus Christ."

One thing is for sure, when GOD starts something, He will complete it. As much as we would love to assist and tell GOD what that process should look like for guaranteed success and completion, His plan is already set. He knows more about us than what we may think. Go ahead and point to yourself and say, "GOD knows me better than I know myself." The assistance GOD desires from each born again believer, is to trust Him and stay the course. It may not be an over-night come through, but when you get to your through, it will be well worth it. We are encouraged to cast all our cares on Him, because He cares for us.

These times in our life can strengthen our character, develop a stronger relationship with the LORD and, make us a living testimony for the kingdom, especially when we allow the work of GOD to be performed in our lives.

Yes, there were times I not only felt like crying, I did cry. I have kept several items that were broken to serve as a reminder of how angry I had gotten. Yes, I felt all alone and wanted to give up and couldn't do so. Deep inside of me, I could feel the push to go through. There was no stopping in the middle and turning back. No matter the circumstance, in the face of opposition, there was a determination to be more than a conqueror and to be victorious in and through JESUS CHRIST.

Guess what? I am still here. There was a strong desire to move forward and a deep driving force within me to push past my obstacles. I am the better for that particular life test. I am a stronger person. I am able to give words of encouragement to others who experience the same thing. My test and trials are examples of hope that if I can make it, so can you. To GOD be all the glory. Without HIM, there is no reasonable way of making it through. It would be better to go through with the LORD, than without Him.

There was a story I had once read, which aided me through the process. Allow me to share. I'll basically paraphrase the narrative, but you will get the message.

Some time ago, two women who lived in the same town and attended the same church had their share of difficulty in life.

One day, a life storm had struck. Both women were devastated. One woman complained every day. Regardless of who she ran into, she did not hold back her displeasure of what was happening to her. Nothing good came out of her mouth, only vile complaints. Everybody knew she was going through. This went on for several years and things only got worse.

However, the other woman who was going through hard times took every opportunity to express how much she loved the LORD. He gave His only Son to give His life for a world destined for hell.

During testimony service, she would offer thanksgiving, praise and adoration to GOD. At home, during her private moments, she would do the same thing, pray and praise the LORD. It wasn't long before this woman realized that GOD had worked things out in her behalf. She testified about it in church.

After church, the woman who always complained approached her and asked why GOD worked it out for her while she herself was still going through? Of course, pleasantly, the grateful woman indulged the complaining woman with this kind response, "Every time I wanted to and attempted to complain or tell GOD how unfair it was to endure this hardship, I remembered what 1 Thessalonians 5:18 said, 'In everything give thanks: for this is the will of GOD in Christ Jesus concerning you.' So, I would tell others about the goodness of JESUS. Although the problem was there, it was by choice to do as the scripture commanded."

No matter what it may look like, through every trial and test, I found myself giving the LORD a praise in the midst of the circumstance. If I'm going to exhaust any energy, I choose to do so in prayer, praise and worship rather than in complaining. I am not saying it is going to be easy and that it will be obstacle free. The same opportunity to complain is the same opportunity to offer praise. I choose to praise.

Reflection:

All of us possess the ability to push past whatever comes our way. There is a fortitude within us, through which when we tap in at just right moment, we take courage. With each new day, no matter the circumstance, if there is breath in our bodies, there is hope.

Often, we may think that some of the things we are experiencing is because the devil is out to get us. We already know that's a fact. Satan does not love us, nor does he like us. The truth be told, the feeling is mutual. There is no love lost here. He desires to sift us as wheat and discredit GOD in our lives.

Our enemy, the devil seeks to display us as an open shame before those who have heard our testimony as one who loves and serves GOD. When we say and express our genuine love for GOD, it will be put to the test. Not only is our love going to be tried, but our faith as well. Through the years of walking with GOD, I learned that if we do not willingly grow or move from one level to the next, we will continue to repeat the same test. Regardless, there is going to be a test, just like a child advancing to the next grade, he or she must pass that current level. This is done by testing the student. However, there is comfort in knowing that the teacher is always present during the test.

The HOLY SPIRIT was and is a keeper. He is a sure Guide. Just like the poem Footprints, when there were only one set of footprints, it was then that the LORD carried HIS child. He wants us to pass every test and trial. He [GOD] is cheering us on. It's good to know that, we are never alone.

No, Never Alone, JESUS promised that He would never leave or forsake us. Be encouraged my friend; this too will pass. Without a doubt, each victory will help us to win other tests.

POINTS TO PONDER
1. Is there a test I keep repeating?

2. Why do I keep repeating the same test?

3. Is this a self-inflicted test or trial?

4. What do I need to do different so that I can pass this test?

5. Are there other tests that I had passed and can use as a reference point?

6. After going through a trial or test, can I say that I am all the better because I have made it through?

7. What is a Scripture I can use to keep me encouraged?

8. Is there one person in whom I trust to pray with and help me be accountable?
9. What am I to learn from and during this test?
10. Am I complaining more than I am praising God?

POINTS TO PRACTICE
1. Pray without ceasing (I Thessalonians 5:17)

2. Those things that concern you, practice casting them upon the LORD.

3. Learn to forgive others and yourself.

4. Do a self-evaluation. There are some behaviors that migrated into our personality that need an eviction

notice. It's time to make some practical adjustments.

5. Whenever you have a dream or vision, write it down. It's alright if you don't understand at that moment, however, do pray and ask GOD to give you clear understanding. When the revelation comes, write it down.

6. Develop a voice of vision of hope. In doing so, one must make a conscious decision to offer praise to GOD instead of complaining to others.

7. With full certainty, know what GOD says about you and speak His words over your life.

8. Practice Philippians 4:8.

9. Be consistent in the things of GOD. Inconsistency is an enemy to our faith. There have been those who had fallen away when times had gotten difficult. It was more than they could bear. When we stay the course, we are demonstrating our trust in GOD.

10. Seek wise and Godly counsel. There is someone that GOD had assigned to each us. When tests/trials come, they can pray with us and for us, hear us out and give us God-centered counsel.

POINTS TO PRAY

Heavenly Father, I thank You for being the keeper of my heart. For You search the heart and know it well. I praise You for Your loving-kindness and tender mercies toward me. Now Father, I know that all thing work together for my good. I love and know that I am called according to Your purpose and plan for my life. You have my best interest at heart. I pray that as I go through this time of testing, You will keep my heart and that I will be better and not bitter. I ask You to allow my tests to become a testimony to help others who may be experiencing trying times. I pray for the peace of GOD to surpass all my understanding and, I take on the mind of Christ as You stretch my faith in You. May I find rest in You and joy in Your comfort. Father GOD, in the name of JESUS, Your Son, may the Holy Spirit be a compass for my soul and lead me in a plain path of righteousness for Your name sake. Do not allow the enemy of my soul to have and take advantage of me when I am vulnerable, but cover, protect me, shield me and guard me in Your care. I'll forever praise and thank You all the days of my life. I am Your servant and Your child, uphold me and keep me. You be glorified in my life. This I pray in the matchless name of JESUS. Amen.

"For I know the thoughts that I think toward you, saith the LORD, thoughts of peace, and not of evil, to give you an expected end." (Jeremiah 29:11 KJV)

4
REJECTED & RESTORED
ELIZABETH RIVERA-WEBB

"AS YOU COME TO HIM, A LIVING STONE REJECTED BY MEN, BUT IN
THE SIGHT OF GOD CHOSEN AND PRECIOUS..."
1 PETER 2:4 (ESV)

The cry and groaning I was hearing appeared to be distant and yet close at the same time. Who was crying so hard? I had not realized that it was coming from me until I felt the stinging tears flow down my cheeks. I was the one crying. Then as suddenly as the tears flowed out and the tightness in my chest swelled, it was all over. I began to feel the release from rejection. I could breathe again. I felt like I had an out of body experience and yet very much aware of my surroundings.

This deliverance conference I attended for the weekend was no joke. I had taken a class offered at our church for all the leaders on deliverance, and I thought, "Well I am okay. What do I need deliverance from?" The preparation leading up to this conference was eight weeks of intense reading and homework. I attended the conference thinking that I was going to get freed from the lack of discipline in my finances and losing weight. Here I was dictating to God what I needed help in. He had other plans for me. God knew exactly where I needed to be delivered. Father always knows best. The speaker asked if there was anyone there that had been suffering from rejection, and he went on about what rejection was and the outcome of it in one's life. I don't even remember going up to the altar for prayer. Something struck me hard about what he said. Mind you, they had covered different things to be delivered from and called them out. When he mentioned "rejection," it was as if a knife went right through my heart.

The walls I had built throughout the years to "protect" myself made sense now. The greatest relief was that I did not have to live in that cage I had built for myself any longer. I could safely come out and enjoy life because for the first time in my life, I realized that I was not alone. I had a defender. I had a Father who protected me. I had a Savior who saved me from my own destruction. His name is Jesus! I experienced Jesus in a way that I had not encountered before. When you think about the meaning of the word "encounter" it means "to come upon unexpectedly, or meet casually; a hostile meeting or conflict." The encounters we have with God may, at times, be unexpected. Sometimes, it can be a hostile meeting if you are boxing with God! In my case, I had been boxing with Him for years, and He won! Every time you have an encounter with God, it marks you, like a permanent tattoo taking you from Glory to Glory! You will never be the same.

During the conference, this was a stage in my life where I was desperately seeking Him for something else, not knowing that He was desperately willing and able to meet me and mark me for life. This was a new side of Him I had never known. It reminded me of the verse in the song Blessed Assurance.

"Blessed assurance Jesus is mine, O what a foretaste of glory divine. Heir of salvation, purchase of God. Born of His Spirit, washed in His blood."

In Jeremiah 29:13, it says, "You will seek me and you will find me when you search for me with all your heart." This is the place I was seeking Him with all my heart. I desperately needed change.

When I went up for prayer, I saw and remembered the first time I experienced rejection and how the emotional pain began.

At about seven years old, I learned very quickly that I needed to defend myself at all costs. My mother was a sitter for about five children from the neighborhood between the ages of six through twelve. During our nap time, the two eldest boys that my mother took care of would touch me in places where no one should be touched. They threatened to do the same to my youngest siblings if I said anything. I took the brunt of it all to protect my siblings. Anger began to take a hold of my young heart and so did rage. I began to build walls of protection. I kept my silence because we needed the money to purchase food and clothing as my father drank and gambled his paychecks away. The abuse continued for two years. No one knew my secret. In the meantime, I displayed outward signs of lashing out at family members, temper tantrums, and isolation.

During my teenage years, I was beginning to show symptoms of a person who has gone through child abuse: low self-esteem, being withdrawn, suicidal thoughts, and abnormal or distorted views of sex.

I was very withdrawn and timid and had low self-esteem to the point that everything had to be perfect. I had to be a straight-A student, or failure would eat me up.

When someone would find something wrong in me, I would have suicidal thoughts. Then I was introduced to pornography by a cousin, and the masturbating began. The anger increased with all the bullying I was getting due to my weight gain, and to top it off, I wore glasses. I had no friends to come over my home, nor was I invited to anyone's home either. God did bring a Christian friend into my life who would be my one friend. I dove into music, journaling, and reading. These were my escape; these were my outlet. I enjoyed singing, writing poems, and journaling my thoughts.

By the age of 16, I reunited with my Christian friend as I had moved to Puerto Rico for about a year and then came back to New York. She invited me to attend her youth service. During this time in my life, my father's drinking had really gotten worse, and he and I resorted to throwing verbal darts at each other. He verbally abused my mom and brothers as well. Usually, he spoke words of negativity into us, words like, "you will never amount to anything, only the rich people make it in life," etc. In his mind, I was doomed to never succeed in anything in life and always be broke.

I accepted the invitation to the youth service with the intent of harming my father when I got back home. I wanted to provoke him to sobriety one way or another, even if it would have cost him his life. I went to the youth service and sat at the last pew. As the youth were up front, worshipping with all their hearts, I had my first encounter with the Lord. I heard His audible voice saying, "Love the sinner, hate the sin." Immediately, I looked around to see who was behind me.

I realized that I was indeed sitting in the last pew and there was no one around me. So, I continued listening to the worship that was going on in front of me, and I heard the same audible voice saying the same thing, "Love the sinner, hate the sin."

After the service, I went home, and my father opened the door to my bedroom instead of kicking it open like he usually did. He was again in his drunken stupor. For the first time in my life, I saw a broken man who needed help. I felt compassion for my dad. I remembered that I was Daddy's girl, and that I loved him. I asked him if he needed anything. Normally, when he kicked my door, I would welcome him with my temper tantrum in full force. Not this time. This startled him. He stood at the doorway of my bedroom just glaring at me as if questioning what was wrong with me. Then he turned around and went into the living room.

A few months later, at a youth choir practice, I accepted Jesus as my personal Savior and Lord, my second encounter. A change began in my life and in my heart. I was so curious as to whom Jesus was. I began to dive into His Word.   I wish I could tell you that my anger simmered down as the years progressed, that I did not hurt anyone in its aftermath or that my self-esteem and other symptoms vanished as soon as I asked the Lord to come into my life. I was a walking time bomb still, waiting to explode on anyone who challenged me or pushed me too far. The words that came out of my mouth would cut through people without knowing how deeply I might have scarred someone.

Yet one of the gifts that He gave me was prophecy. I did not want it. I told the Lord to use someone else.

In His mercy, God used many people to come alongside me and bring to my attention what I was not seeing in myself. They confronted me with issues like how to be more tactful with my words, how to soften the way I spoke to others, and how to be mindful of my facial expressions. Instead of me asking God to help me in this area, I took offense and became even more secluded. I cried bitter tears because I felt I was disappointing God and cried out to Him for change.

I began to really search the scriptures, and the Holy Spirit began to confirm what others were telling me. He showed me a scripture that I would diligently pray and still do.

Colossians 4:6 says, *"Let your speech always be gracious, seasoned with salt, so that you may know how you ought to answer each person."*

The Holy Spirit has a way of speaking truth to us through the revelation of His Scripture that results in change. Only He can do that! I began to ask the Lord to search my heart and show me. He did just what I requested and revealed to me how I was speaking along with my motives. I responded with obedience and submission to His revelation of the condition of my heart and emotions. The Lord began using me in worship, teaching, and prophesying.

Suddenly, life seemed to shoot daggers at me with the death of my mother, disappointments in relationships, lack of being a good steward of my finances, trust issues, insecurities, etc. Anger started to creep back in because at this point, I began to get angry at God. I was annoyed that I had prayed for others who were healed or delivered, yet I had been asking GOD for years to deliver me from rage and other issues, but nothing. Initially, it all came from being mad at my father for drinking and not protecting me, so as the disappointments came, the layers of walls deepened and thickened.

Because I am a survivor and a go-getter, I had the appearance of having it together, but inside, I was secretly building walls. Every time someone rejected me, I built a wall. Every time I didn't get accolades that I felt I needed, I built a wall. Every time I was corrected by leadership, I built a wall. Every time the Holy Spirit reminded me of all my wrongs, I built a wall because I failed God. Secretly, I was holding my fist up at God and asking him why, "I pray. I read the Bible. I am obedient. I go to every service. I pray for people. I disciple others. Why God? Why are these things happening to me? Why are you not protecting me from all this pain?" I did not feel loved. Yet I knew deep inside of me that He did love me. He promised to work it all out for my good like His Word says.

Now, in my 40's, I found myself in this deliverance conference on the last day, and the facilitator started speaking on overcoming rejection. He said that rejection is the absence of love. That struck a chord in me. In our booklet, there was a scripture from Isaiah 41:9 that reads, "I have chosen you and have not rejected you." The word "chosen" always humbled me. I am chosen? Me? Are you sure? The speaker began to explain what walls were and the different layers. As he read every layer, I could relate to each, for I had built them throughout the years of my life.

The walls he categorized are:

1. Rejection of God – not putting your faith in the Word of God and waiting on Him.
2. Self-rejection – disliking ourselves because we fail God and others.
3. Fear of rejection – trying to hide away from God and others. You become isolated. Some go to the other extreme and become pleasers of men or perfectionists.
4. Rejection of others – fault finders and blaming others.

Oh, how this reminded me of Adam and Eve when they realized they had sinned against God. All God told them to do was not eat from the tree of the knowledge of good and evil (Gen. 2:15-17). Eve decides to venture out into the garden and decides to listen to the serpent (Gen. 3:1) instead of "putting her faith in the Word of God and what He told her." She bites into the fruit. Eve then proceeds to share this experience with her husband where he also indulges in taking a bite (Gen. 3:6-7).

They must have figured, "well, we are both still standing. We are not struck dead like God said. Hooray!" Suddenly, they hear the Father's footsteps approaching (Gen.3:8), and before the familiar sound of His voice summons them, self-rejection fills their hearts and minds. A new dislike for themselves derives from their disobedience to God.

They failed Him. As the Father's presence moves closer to them, they experience the formation of another layer of the wall – fear of rejection. Adam and Eve tried to hide. Seriously? You cannot hide from God. What were they thinking? In verse 12, Adam blames Eve and God: "The woman **You** put here with me, gave me some fruit from the tree and I ate it." The other wall was built – rejection of others.

As I stood before the person who was going to pray for my deliverance, I felt someone hold me. It wasn't the person praying for me because she barely touched my forehead, and it surely wasn't the person behind me. The Lord Himself comforted me. I was relieved that on this day, freedom was going to be mine. She led me into a prayer of renouncing and repenting for the walls I had built, and then she prayed. Sincerely, I can say that from that day forward, I have been free of rejection, for I was introduced to LOVE in its truest form. I have never lacked love since. My relationships changed with people.

I wasn't as needy or dependent on others. My confidence level increased because I now knew whose daughter I was. I smiled more and became friendlier. I allowed hugs, and I gave them. I began to love people genuinely and see them like God sees them. My speech and countenance changed as well. I no longer stood on excuses like: this was the way I was made; I inherited my mother's face; either you like me, or you don't. All excuses were gone. I want people to see Jesus flowing out of me. I want what He desires to say to be what I communicate with His authority and grace. I experienced a compassion for God's people on a whole different level where I would cry out for their souls. The thoughts of suicide and *lust had been dealt with way before this encounter with the Lord at this conference. That may be the next chapter I write. Stay tuned.

I returned home from the conference thanking God so much for His grace and for His mercy and love towards me. My life could have turned out in various ways.

Prior to my encounter with Jesus, my temper boiled to the point that I knew I could end up in jail easily for murdering someone. Yet instead, God desired to have encounters with me that would mark me and change me forever.

Beloved, God has a better plan for us than we could ever imagine. Unbelievably, I thought I had the ability to dictate to the Lord what I needed to be delivered from, yet He dug deeper and went straight to the root of it. **He touched me** by revealing the error of my ways. **He changed** me through the power of His Word, and **He made me whole** by keeping me from turning back to the way I used to be. Although the enemy had made efforts to tempt me and test my deliverance, I have stood on God's Word, and His Spirit has empowered me to receive wholeness in this area.

In the past, I had been accused because of how I used to speak to people, and some would say that I did not care for people. During these times, when I was in front of leadership, the Lord Himself would calmly still my heart and spirit and speak gently, "Do not say a word. I am your defense." I submitted to authority, and I did not act like I used to. My prayer was and is that I project the love of Christ always, in every situation, and that His character will be demonstrated through my life. In order to do that, I must refuse to hold onto grudges or resentments. I asked the Lord to show me ahead of time the traps the enemy set before me. Most of the time, He does, but there have been occasions upon which I was blindsided and caught off guard. Those are the moments when the Lord shines through me the best. I quickly and immediately seek and ask for forgiveness from God or anyone I may have offended. I do not wait because that gives room for the seeds of offense to fester in my heart and in the other person. "If at all possible be at peace with everyone" (Romans 12:18). There is one book that has truly been second to my Bible, and that is *The Bait of Satan* by John Bevere. I read it every year to keep my heart and emotions pure.

POINTS TO PRAY

Father God loves us so much that He wants us to grow in Him. He invites you to go deeper in your walk with Him. Remember the enemy comes to steal, and to kill, and to destroy. But God has come so that you may have life, and that you may have it in abundance (John 10:10). As you read this chapter, ask yourselves these questions:

1. What walls have I built that are stopping me from progressing in the Lord?
   a. Rejection of God
   b. Self-rejection
   c. Fear of rejection
   d. Rejection of others

2. What things have disappointed me to the point of being angry and bitter with God, myself, and others?

3. How do I react when God highlights areas in my life that need change? Do I seek Him for deliverance or run from Him?

4. Do I get offended when God brings others to speak truth into my life?

POINTS TO PRACTICE

1. Ask the Lord to search your heart daily. If He finds anything that is not pleasing to Him, ask Him to reveal it to you. Don't be afraid when He does. He is capable of showing you the necessary steps towards freedom (Psalm 139:23-24). Pursue it! Allow change to happen.

2. Be open to those brave men and women of God that the Lord puts in your path to let you know that change is needed. Do not shut them out. The Lord uses them as warnings to guide us and help us to see truth about ourselves that we may, otherwise, not be able to see (Prov. 11:14).

3. Look up scriptures that will help you to be accountable to His Word. When I needed to change the way I spoke to people, one Scripture I found was Colossians 4:6: "Let your conversation be always full of grace, seasoned with salt, so that you may know how to answer everyone."

4. Be accountable to someone. Do not isolate yourself. Have an individual who you can trust to pray and stand with you.

5. Stay free! You do this by bringing into captivity every thought, every emotion, and every feeling that is not from God (2 Cor. 10:5). Submit to His Word, recognize the sin, repent, and renounce it. Then, walk in His grace and mercy.

POINT TO PRAY

Beloved, if you have come to the place where the Lord has highlighted an area or areas in your heart that need dealing with, will you say this prayer with me?

*"Dear heavenly Father, please forgive me for giving place to anger [**or whatever you are facing right now**]. I am sorry for partnering up with anger [**or whatever you are facing right now**] instead of trusting You. I call this sin. I repent of all known or unknown generational sins, and I ask for Your forgiveness to flow through all generations of my family. Thank you for Your forgiveness and destroying all the walls that I have built separating me from You. I ask You to break every wall and every yoke of bondage from my life in Jesus' name. I accept You as Lord over all those areas where I have built a wall.*

*I renounce anger [**or whatever you are facing right now**] in my life, as well as any other spirit known or unknown to me that has cooperated with the enemy's plan.*

*I declare this day that I will be free from your power. I refuse to accept your influences in my life any longer. In the name of Jesus, I close all doors that I have opened to anger [**or whatever you are facing right now**] in my life, and I pull* *down every stronghold you have erected in my soul. I take back all the ground given to you in the mighty name of Jesus.*

*Lord, I pray for a fresh outpouring of your Holy Spirit over the place that anger [**or whatever you renounced**] has occupied. I ask you, Holy Spirit, to invade and possess this new territory. I invite You to rule and reign and be Lord over this place. May you bless me with boldness and confidence to trust You. In Jesus name! Amen."*

5

THE SHAME OF SILENCE
LISA JOHNSON

This is the first time I am telling this story. For years, shame kept me silent. The silence kept me bound. The decision to be free caused me to do things I have never done before, which includes telling my story on such a large stage. But fear is a defeated enemy, right?

I was in my early 20's when I had a procedure done. It is not something I am proud of or ever want to do again! During this time in my life, I was searching for who I was and trying to be everything I saw others do and be. All my life, I have been teased and walked on like a mat. In grade school, on the yellow bus, the kids would call me "tick face" because I had a severe case of acne that refused to clear up regardless of the various doctors and treatments I tried.

I remember feeling so ugly when I was a teenager. One particular Saturday, I placed a paper bag on my head. The acne and black scars that covered my face made it difficult to see my caramel/toffee skin tone underneath.

On that day, my dad encouraged me saying that I was beautiful despite what anyone else said. I smiled for the moment, but still, deep inside, I was disappointed and wanted to just give up.

I remember crying constantly because I did not know how to make myself beautiful inside and out. I carried this with me into my late 20's and early 30's. Ridding myself of acne has been my own personal war zone. I believed no one would see the beauty within me because they could not get pass my outward appearance and that I wouldn't find a man who would love me. So of course, finally, when someone did give me attention, I clung to it and refused to let go. I doubted that I would ever experience it again. This mindset pushed me to accept things that were below my standards and character. I accepted verbal and mental abuse from guys who were controlling and manipulating because I did not know my self-worth. I had not yet learned that I was beautifully and wonderfully made. (Psalms 139.14)

One day, I met a gentleman, whom we will call Jerome, at the bus station of all places. Still, I have no idea why or how I was attracted to this person. I remember questioning my giving him the time of day. Have you ever had those moments when you asked yourself, "what was I thinking?" That was mine! Although Jerome was nice looking, he didn't have anything really going for himself. He worked at the bus station and was in the process of relocating to the area where I resided. He stayed with his aunt. He didn't even have a driver's license! What in the world was I thinking?!

We dated for a short time of less than six months. When I introduced him to my mother and father, he was so nonchalant and even disrespected my dad. My father asked him a question, and he just shrugged his shoulders and threw his hands up. Throughout the visit, he looked away, stared out in the distance, and refused to show interest in anything my father had to say.

One would think this would have been a BIG clue that this person was not the one for me. Duh! Nope.

I continued dating and hanging out with him because I was receiving the attention that I always wanted. I ignored some signs because he seemed like he was really interested in me. One day, we were at his aunt's house, and we had intercourse for the first time. It was awkward because I knew this was wrong, but I kept going. It was like I was not even there. When it was over, I asked him if he had used any protection. He said he had, but I knew he was lying. It was strange, but immediately, I knew I was pregnant. Jerome left the room and didn't return. I got really scared and was thinking, "What am I going to do now that I am pregnant? How do I take care of a child? What will my parents say and/or do? What will people say if I have a child outside of marriage?" A strong spirit of fear came over me:

I can still vividly remember sobbing and being terribly frightened, but I managed to get myself together and went to the living room where his aunt was. With a sureness that came from deep within, I told her this would be the last time she would see me, and that it was a pleasure meeting her. She asked me several times what I meant. She was quite concerned and appeared nervous by my words because she could see I was not alright. I repeated myself, and I left out the house, got in my car, and went home. I withdrew myself from Jerome and did not return any of his calls. I remember getting a pregnancy test and the results confirmed my previous assumption was accurate. I was pregnant!

One day, I had a vision that demons and imps were jumping in and out of the hood of my car constantly and that they were just torturing me. Carrying around this secret was tormenting me. I kept my pregnancy hidden from my parents for approximately two months. Then, I finally confided in my dad. When I told my dad I was pregnant, he supported and encouraged me.

We sat down and talked about the possibility of keeping my baby, but I said no; I did not want my child brought up in an environment where we both made immature decisions, knowing Jerome could not be the father my child needed. And quite frankly, real talk, I was petrified!

As a result, my father and I agreed that I would have an abortion.

My father wanted me to get funds from Jerome to pay for the procedure, but I declined. I did not want anything else to do with him, and I never shared with him that I aborted his child.

My dad said this would be our secret, and we would not say anything to anyone, not even my mom. To this day, my mother still doesn't know I had an abortion. We were afraid and ashamed of what people would say and how they might have reacted if they knew what we had done. I was imprisoned by secrecy. The torment continued.

It's important to understand that the enemy wants to keep people held hostage with the shame and guilt of their past. Inadvertently, this can lower self-esteem. Remember, the enemy came to kill, steal, and destroy by any means necessary (John 10:10).

I can remember in detail the day I went to the facility for the procedure. I can still see the various faces of the other young girls who were there. I overheard one of them say they were not ready to settle down and have children of their own. She said this was her fifth abortion. When I heard this, I cringed, and my heart went out to her. I wondered to myself how anyone could do this so many times as if it's as simple as going to the bathroom. I was torn. When it was finally my turn to see the doctor, they did an ultrasound. The nurse was quite nasty and rude towards me. They began the procedure for a pap smear. It was one of the most painful pap smears, I have ever had.

The cold words she spoke next stung as if she had just slapped me right in the face, "You were not hurting when you got pregnant!" She rudely stated. I was too embarrassed and broken to respond. I really wanted to scream, "You don't know what happened to me! What if I was raped? Would you say the same thing?"

The nurse continued with the ultrasound, and I began to have an unexpected excitement about this human being inside of me. There was a natural curiosity.

I wanted to see my baby on the screen and know its sex. "Was it a boy or a girl?" Whether the nurse detected my growing wonderment or not, I don't know, but as if just for spite, the nurse turned the screen away from me. I was not able to see. Deep down, I was crying out for help and for someone to come and say it was going to be okay. I wanted someone to offer me options and tell me what could be done to fix this situation, but that didn't happen.

Afterwards, my dad and I drove home in complete silence. Before we got out of the car, my dad coached me to make certain that I didn't show any sign of discomfort or sickness. "Keep your head up," he instructed. I did just what he said, but every night when I was all alone, I sobbed silently to myself until I drifted to sleep. This process began the coverup where I successfully learned to mask the real me and put on a fake face for everyone else to see. Just like that Saturday morning when I put a bag over my head; I was looking for ways to hide the torment inside. From that moment on, whenever I would see children or be around them, I was tortured.

I would see the ugly, scary faces of demons in front of a child, and I would hear a taunting voice say that the child would not like me. This went on for some years to the point where I would just go the opposite way whenever I would see children.

I have always loved children and children have loved me. Yet after the abortion, that changed. It took many years of deliverance for me to reconnect and love children the way I had before.

I was miserable. During this time, I went to church but had no power. I knew who Jesus was and how to pray but that was it. I remember around age 25, I realized there had to be more and started searching for more of God.

In the most amazing way, I found him. I switched congregations and God sent me a prophetic worship liturgical dancer mentor. He used her to lead me to Christ, and I was filled with the Holy Spirit. I learned how to walk in the power and authority God had given me. It changed everything and was the best thing that ever happened to me. Alleluia!!! God used dance to heal me of rejection, low self-esteem, unforgiveness, hatred and bitterness. I danced, swayed and stomped away the pain that was locked within for so long. I received a new means of expression and communication. Each movement was like a breath of fresh air. It was as if He was breathing new life through every flick of my flag and each twirl brought me closer into His embrace.

During one of our worship sessions, God performed a major deliverance in me. He started at my present age of 35 and took me back to the tender age of two, telling and showing me the things that I suffered in my life, and all the while, He was healing, delivering, and restoring ALL!

My heavenly Father conveyed to me in this session that my mother planned to abort me. My biological father had been on drugs. When I heard this, God revealed this was a generational curse.

The gentleman I was dating also looked just liked my biological father and had similar traits.

How interesting. From that moment, the generational curse of abortion was broken off of me, and I received God's healing. Now began the process of complete forgiveness for my mom, myself, my dad, and Jerome. I was rejected, bitter, and judgmental. I possessed hatred for men, but was still trying to find acceptance because of rejection.

God asked me to write a letter to my mom and tell her that I love her. I found this quite challenging because we never had a "normal" mother-daughter relationship. I held resentment toward her. I remember one day, we had friends and family over, and we were all at the table while talking about children and how they all had them. I was the youngest at the table. Everyone else was in their mid to upper forties.

My mom yelled out, "I never want you to have kids!" She was looking directly at me. The house grew silent. The faces around the table were filled with shock and surprise. That statement pierced my heart to the core. I got up quietly and went in my room and cried. My dad came in and tried to comfort me. I asked him, "How could she say this?"

I told him that I should go out and get pregnant now and show her that I can have children! He encouraged me not to do something like that because it was the wrong motive. When I went back to ask my mom why she would say such a thing, she acted as if it never happened, and she looked like a deer in headlights. Seemingly, she did not even care.

GOD took me on a journey where I had to deal with unforgiveness, rejection, hatred, bitterness, and low self-esteem so I could be rid of the baggage and walk in confidence, strength, power, authority, and respect. God instructed me to write a letter to my mom and to forgive her. Writing this letter required arduous effort and took several months for me to work up the courage to finally sit down and write. God pushed me and would not relent. I heard him say, "It must be done!"

Because God forgives willingly and fully, we must do the same. We are told in Matthew 6:14-15: "For if you forgive other people when they sin against you, your Heavenly Father will also forgive you. But if you do not forgive others their sins, your Father will not forgive your sins". I fought God and truly did not want to write this letter to my mom. I remember sitting on my bed weeping as I heard the audible voice of God encouraging me that with His help, I could do this, so I could move on.

He told me to write some positive things about my mom and some things she does well. I told God there was nothing good to write about my mom and threw my pen down in frustration. Holy Spirit was such a gentleman; He spoke with a soft, quiet voice, "Now pick up the pen, dig deep, and find something positive about your mom." Out of my love for God and my desire to obey, I began to write.

To my surprise, there were a lot of positives about my mom that I had not realized before (because of the pain that blinded me from seeing). I wrote about how she was a good cook, how she made sure I had the necessities, and how she ensured that I had the best teachers and tutors for my education. This letter was at least two and a half pages long. I cried through the whole process because Holy Spirit showed me how much my mom does care and love me. She did the best she knew to do. From that point, Holy Spirit led me to lay down any grudges and resentment I held towards my mom and release her back to Him. This brought a feeling of freedom that I hadn't previously known. A million pounds lifted off my shoulders. I stand amazed at God's ability to redeem and rescue His people. Amen!

Once I finished the letter, I was directed to throw the letter away. "What? Why?" I thought. Quite confused by this, I questioned, "Why?" I had assumed the next step would be to mail it to her. "No," was the heavenly reply I received, "this was just for you to process and forgive your mother."

I agreed and said I understood. Holy Spirit then advised me that I would have to do the same for my biological dad. I fought even harder not to do this because I had such hatred for this man.

He left me when I was two years old, and I only saw him once more when I was 16 at his mother's funeral. He told me he would write, and I could come visit, but it never happened. He lied, and I was hurt and mad. Holy Spirit pressed upon my heart to write the letter, and I was fighting hard against it, but Holy Spirit knows best and didn't give up on me. It took me about two weeks to finally sit down and write this letter. This time, it was easier to write this letter of forgiveness. Again, I am in my bed writing this letter lead by Holy Spirit when He tells me to write some positives about my father. I told Him that I didn't have any because he had not been in my life since I was two years old. Holy Spirit told me to dig deeper.

As I began to dig deeper, I found myself expressing all the frustration and hurt I held towards him while at the same time I told him that I forgave him and asked him to forgive me for my actions. At the end of this letter, I was instructed to write an invitation for repentance, salvation, healing, and deliverance for him. At the completion of this letter, I was again in awe of God. I started off bitter and angry and then turned around asking for forgiveness and giving an invitation to receive Christ. WOW! What took me two hours to pen lifted a lifetime of weight off of me. All that bondage and those chains of rejection, hatred, bitterness, and unforgiveness were broken in the name of Jesus!

I believe many people need to experience God's freedom and His peace that comes from it. I would like to take this time to invite you to lay down your burdens and experience the liberation that I experienced. Let's take a minute right now to repent for any unforgiveness, hatred, or grudges you may have. It's time to let them go.

Ask Holy Spirit to come into your heart and break the bondage and chains of rejection, self-hatred, suicide, bitterness, unforgiveness, low self-esteem, people pleasing, anger, abuse of all kinds, control, and manipulation. I Command them to be broken, demolished, and no longer accepted by the person reading this, in Jesus' name.

Now, ask Holy Spirit for an encounter with Him that will fill you with power, love, peace, confidence, strength, encouragement, a sound mind, right and positive relationships with divine intervention, and guidance in Jesus' name.

Since this time, I have continued to seek God through His word and through dance. Through the pain, I birthed forth *Intimacy N' Worship Ministries* in 2010. The pain, suffering, and unforgiveness forced me closer to God because He was the only one who could save and deliver me from the enemy – the inner me. Selah.

POINTS TO PONDER

1. How much God loves you

2. How a small offense can hurt, delay, block, and even destroy you or your destiny

3. God's forgiveness and how it heals and delivers you from bondage, sickness, low self-esteem, bitterness, offense, etc. Read & meditate on Mark 11:25, Ephesians 4:32, Matthew 6:15, 1 John 1:9

4. God is so in love with you that He knows your every thought. He knows all the hairs on your head. He is our deliverer and our healer. What an awesome God we serve. Matthew 10:27-31

5. He is the Alpha and Omega. The beginning and the end. Our redeemer. Our Peacemaker. Our strong tower. Our Father. He is the lifter of our head.

6. Psalm 139:1-- You are beautifully and wonderfully made.

7. Philippians 4:13-- I can do all things through Christ who strengthens me.

POINTS TO PRACTICE

1. Ask Holy Spirit to reveal to you who you must forgive.

2. Seek the Lord to show you any offense that caused you to be bitter, angry, mean, disrespectful, resentful, etc.

3. Now repent for holding on to all these things; ask Holy Spirit to break these weights off of you and release yourself from the offense. Next, confess aloud that you receive God's forgiveness, and that you forgive the ones who hurt you as well as yourself.

4. Continue by requesting in prayer for all wounds to be healed and sealed with the glory of God and to be filled up with His joy, peace, love, gentleness, long suffering... the fruit of the spirit in Jesus' name.

POINT TO PRAY

Now, ask the Lord to fill you with His glory and power and give you a desire to win souls for His Kingdom. Pray with passion, thirst and hunger for the power of God to come in and for His word to come alive in you with clarity. Seek Him for understanding, peace, and love.

Now receive your blessing of ALL of what you just prayed. Continue to forgive daily and watch God heal and deliver you from all the hurt, abuse, hatred, bitterness, etc. in Jesus name. God Bless!

6
HERE WE GO AGAIN
TAMIKU THOMPSON

Rejected! It started in the womb and progressed throughout my childhood. At the age of nine or ten, I remember one Christmas Eve; my siblings had gifts wrapped under the tree, but I didn't see anything with my name on it. Christmas morning came, and I was handed a "Steinmart" bag from my stepfather with a shirt inside. A shirt?! I was stunned as I watched my brothers look with glee and excitement as they tore through the wrapping paper that covered their plastic army action figures, toy pistols with holsters, and Tonka trucks. I sat there crushed and felt as though I didn't belong.

No hugs, no kisses, no words of affirmation; it became obviously clear my mother was experiencing her own issues and heartaches that kept her from connecting with me. Looking at other children receive the love that I yearned for left my innocent spirit feeling battered and bruised. Maybe my mother didn't want me or had intended to abort me or simply didn't know what to do with me. I don't know, but a major milestone in my life came when I learned, "hurting people hurt others." My journey of wanting to be accepted and loved drove me to many unwarranted places and took on various faces where I found myself emotionally, physically, sexually, and spiritually wounded.

Rejection and abandonment raised its ugly head and stayed with me for many years. School was hard as I worked to fit in. I carried my feelings as if in a backpack, lugging this baggage everywhere I went.

During the formative years where others are establishing relationships, I didn't fit in. I found myself awkward and usually alone. First, my religious upbringing meant I dressed differently; while the other girls wore pants in the winter, I wore dresses and leg warmers. Of course, my clothing styles caused me to be the target of their sneers, jokes, and name-calling. I recall one time, while I was walking home from school, several classmates followed behind me, taunting me with an Al Green song, "I Want Me a Sanctified Lady." I can laugh at it now and even see a compliment in it, but then, it left me feeling further alienated.

Sometimes, I fought hard to be one of the so called "cool kids." I played along with what my classmates deemed amusing at the expense of others. This was short-lived, because they would always turn it back on me. I would then find myself at the end of their cruel jokes, which wasn't funny at all. Secondly, I wasn't very good at sports. I recall during P.E., we would play games where team captains would pick their teams. I hoped and waited for my name to be called, but usually, I was selected by default. Things like this stripped me of the confidence that I could be the best at what I set my mind to do. Finally, when I thought I had friends who liked me, I realized that they only came around when I had money. Several times, my money came up missing, and after I put two and two together, I realized that it was stolen by my "so called" friends. I know that many children have had challenges at school, but they usually have the reprieve of going home to find comfort. However, for me, home was just as daunting as school.

Not only was there a void in the place of a mother's love, but I also had the compounded issue of a missing father. The only thing that I knew about my biological father was what I dreamt up in my mind. I envisioned him being a loving man who would wrap his arms around me while listening to my problems and giving me fatherly advice, full of wisdom. In actuality, he was a stranger and someone I never got a chance to meet. My daddy was absent, but the craving for love became more present. I'm not certain if my father even knew I existed.

Whether this was by his choice or my mother's, I'm not sure. Whenever I approached the subject with my mother, I didn't receive many answers. It appears that the only encounter between him and my mom was the night I was conceived. Therefore, that was that.

When you cannot find love at home, you look for it in other places. I sought it out in church. Typically, when a person thinks of church, they think of the love and acceptance that is found in the house of God. For a while, this was true for me as well. After not having a choice in attending church, I realized how much I loved going. It became my sanctuary, escape, and place of refuge. I finally felt like I belonged. The emptiness and sadness that pestered and pounced upon me was lifted when I entered those doors. One mistake changed all of that.

I grew up in a faith that rightly believed that people should remain virgins until marriage. However, that was all that I was taught about sex and intimacy. The bulk of our sex education was simply "Don't Do It!" Although we were taught that we should not fornicate or commit adultery, I received mixed messages. The message was clear from the pulpit, however, it was confusing from the pew. I heard it in my ear, but what I saw and experienced was different. There were musicians who were engaging young women in compromising ways, and in one instance, a lady ended up pregnant. I was the victim of being inappropriately touched by one of the Deacons as well. I was traumatized to the point that I disliked a man with a beard, because it brought back horrible memories of times his prickly facial hair rubbed against my delicate skin as he invaded my mouth with his toothless gums. I'm sure that I wasn't the only child that his perverted hands touched. Knowing it was wrong yet seeing those who say they loved God give into their lustful and fleshly desires caused greater confusion in my young mind.

In addition, I could have benefited from more information on how to abstain from sex and how to honor marriage. I needed to know where I could find the self-control when hormones, peer pressure, and life were vigorously unfolding. Unfortunately, sex was a taboo subject. Many people understand the importance of teenagers entering puberty and the need of their parents and religious establishments to train and mentor them in this area, because having experienced the damage of ignorance, sent me into oblivion without having the proper guidance.

At home, my family barely talked about anything closely related to sex. My siblings and I were excused from adult conversations, and if anything, hardly related to intimacy came on television, we were told to cover our eyes. Of course, my mother and stepfather reminded us to just stay a virgin until marriage. Although I was not popular with the girls at school, there came a time when I became the center of attraction for the boys. Unbeknownst to me, I was the prey and the object of the game, "Pop the Cherry." Making it home safely became a laborious task. I desired attention, but the courting, friendly, and loving kind, not the type that was lustful. I thought I was good at running and was winning the game until I found myself in the wrong place at the wrong time.

Here, simply saying "no" did not work. This traumatic encounter resulted with me discovering that I was pregnant at sweet sixteen. Wow, even now, it's hard to say: I WAS RAPED by my next-door neighbor! But that is exactly what happened. I struggled with identifying the exonerating details of what transpired, because I begin to equate this form of force with love. The idea that someone else was getting pleasure at my expense caused me to silence my yells and go with the flow. After the initial rape, I endured ceaseless abusive encounters until I finally left home and joined the military.

My body had become his property, the place where he released his aggression. I begin to accept this kind of treatment as the norm. I teetered between "does he love me?" and "this is abuse" until my eyes were illuminated. Not only was my body abused, but psychologically, I was battered as well. The shame, guilt, and feelings of failure left me thinking that God plagued me mixed with a looming feeling of low self-esteem. This opened the door to promiscuity.

Not too long after my neighbor had his way with me, I left to visit relatives in Chicago. It was during this time I began noticing that my body was changing. Sixteen and pregnant. NO! This couldn't be happening to me. The fear of me being pregnant had me on pins and needles. I would wake up in the mornings and go to bed at night, crossing my fingers and hoping that it was not true. Crossing my fingers didn't change my missed period. I tried to continue with life, convincing myself that it was just my mind playing tricks on me. I finally had to come to grips with the truth. Life was different and different couldn't be ignored. As if the dizzy spells weren't enough, I had a church member, Sis. Barbara, pull me and my mother aside and ask me point blank if I was pregnant. I was forced to connect with my truth and there was no denying it. I was pregnant, so I set the appointment for my first prenatal visit.

Because of what I endured, I made a determination about this baby growing in my womb. My baby would be loved and wanted! I was told to not tell who got me pregnant, and someone even recommended that I get an abortion. This suggestion brought me full circle to my own pain of abandonment and rejection. When I told the baby's father that I was expecting, I wanted some level of acceptance, but didn't get that. I thought, "Here I go again, looking for something that wasn't there." Not only was I rejected by the man who had gotten me pregnant, but I was also rejected by the church. Talk about triple-body blows.

"My God, my God, why hast thou forsaken me? why art thou so far from helping me, and from the words of my roaring?" Psalms 22:1 (KJV)

I could understand how Jesus must have felt being around people so long who seemed like they had his back only to hear them utter the words, "crucify him." I was devastated as I could relate in some ways to this story. My church home that had become family gave up on me too.

To the best of my ability, I had lived my life doing what was expected and told to do. I had asked Christ into my life at a young age, got baptized with water and fire, served in the sunshine band (the children's choir), and even graduated to the green and white robes (the adult choir). I did so with gladness. This was a proud moment because our choir would sing you off your pew at any program or church convention. Even as a teenager, I had ushered in all white, took communion, paid my tithes from any increase, took care of and greatly respected the elderly.

I knew that I had to give honor to the Pastor, pulpit guest, everyone in the congregation, and God at the beginning of any words that I had to say on a program. I had invested my time in taking care of others, including my family, so I just did not understand what was to follow. After all, none but the righteous shall see God...right? I was being removed from the choir and abruptly stopped from fellowships with my church friends. Deep inside myself I questioned this string of distasteful occurrences.

I had shared many fun moments with them, like playing a mean tambourine or engaging in games like hopscotch. These activities faded out to include no overnight sleepovers at their homes, because I was considered "fast" and "unclean." The only difference is, while I was running from somebody's arms, some of the other girls were running towards a boy's arm. It was as if I was wearing a bold letter "S" on my forehead and I do not mean "S" for Superwoman. There was no one to hear my side of the story or who cared to hear my explanation. It appeared to me that I was being sentenced to the outer tent when news broke that I was with child. I was isolated, abandoned, and rejected! Talk about self-esteem issues along with the feelings of your heart being ripped right out of your chest - this totally crushed me!

I gave birth to a beautiful, bouncy, and healthy baby girl on February 20th of 1988 at 9:13am in a cold, dark hospital room in Mississippi. Overcoming the excruciating pain of childbirth as a young teenager with no hand to hold would have been a suitable reason to give up, but there was a hidden, mighty strength working on the inside of me. I had no epidural or pain medicine. I experienced natural childbirth without an epidural or pain medication, mixed with the fear of the unknown. After delivering my sweet baby, the contractions continued, so for a moment, I wondered if there was another baby waiting to be born.

There was more than a sigh of relief when the doctor revealed to me that it was only the afterbirth being expelled from my body. Throughout my pregnancy, labor and delivery, I felt alone and clueless, because no one was there to teach or help me transition from life as a teenage girl to motherhood. This was another stage in my life in which I felt abandoned by the ones who should have been there to nurture and care for me. However, I now know that God's hand was upon me and He comforted me through these hardships.

Years later, after becoming a mother, I became more aware of a parent's impact. Even as an adult, I still wanted to connect with my father. My heart yearned to meet and know my dad. On a visit back home, my uncle did a little investigation of his own. After talking with the one he suspected to be my biological father, my uncle passed a phone number to me. I guess my biological father told him that if I wanted to talk, the ball was in my court. Finally, I mustered up the courage to call. I did it! However, my hopes to connect with my father came to a screeching halt that day. I called, wanting to at least hear his voice for the first time, but instead, a young man answered the phone.

Apprehensively, I asked to speak with the man I presumed to be my dad. The reply I received on the other end of the phone took me from a state of living my dream to experiencing a nightmare.

The young man said, "We've just left his funeral service today." He then passed the phone to another male that announced himself as the son of the deceased and asked me about my identity. How would I receive answers or closure now? The conversation was short, and he said that he would get back to me, but that never happened. Instead of a call, I received rumors. Rumors circulated that I was seeking some form of fortune or just simply out of my mind. WHAT?!Here again, I reached out to find answers, closure, or maybe, just possibly to be loved, but I found myself in a cycle of rejection.

However, this time there was a new dynamic in place. I had gained a new level of spiritual maturity. Though the information shocked and hurt a little, it did not send me into a state of depression that had become familiar. I was amazed at how the Holy Spirit walked me through that ordeal. There is a known saying I thought about, "You can't miss what you never had," but I realized more and more that this was not true. I had missed what I didn't have, but the Lord was filling the void in my heart.

Here we go again... As you can see, I experienced ostracism from individuals and groups through which most people find the greatest acceptance. From all of this, I was almost convinced the many retakes would exclude me from fulfilling my God ordained purpose.

I came to a point in my life where I realized that temporary thrills were not satisfactory for me, and besides that, they were very costly! Looking for love in all the wrong places led me to be betrayed by my best friend who, while being "friendly" with me, introduced her sister to my fiancé who he then ended up marrying.

In addition, I had a miscarriage. I contemplated suicide, but God intervened. This drove me to seek God in a new way.

It pushed me to move out of my surroundings, and I left the state to start over. I contemplated going back home to Mississippi, but after praying and thinking hard about my options, I decided I would press forward and not go backwards.

I solidified this decision with a physical relocation to Colorado in 1999. After I moved, I still wasn't delivered, and the drama followed me - another guy with a different name and face. During this time, I also went through financial attacks that ended with a bankruptcy.

Nevertheless, I wanted to surrender all and was being pulled back to my first love. You see, often what we think is good for us is not what God has for us. I made a conscious decision to let my current lifestyle and surroundings go. I wanted peace of mind and more of Jesus.

I attended several denominational churches until I ended up in a non-denominational prophetic ministry that assisted me in confronting God's Word and applying it to my daily life. I enrolled in what was intended to be a year commitment to a spiritual ministry developmental training. It ended up being much, much longer than that. I knew I needed to be removed from man's tradition and truly know God for myself.

I learned many lessons from my encounters through personal and close relationships; yet, my advance lessons came from church leaders. I honored what the Bible says about entreating those who have rule over you.

My desire was to make it easy for those who shepherd me. I allowed my leaders to pour into my spirit the truth from God's Word and teach me how to seek His Word out for myself so I could be renewed and transformed into His image. There were images that needed to be destroyed by what others thought of me and what I believed about myself. The following Scriptures helped to sever the lying perceptions of the enemy.

"And be not conformed to this world: but be ye transformed by the renewing of your mind, that ye may prove what is that good, and acceptable, and perfect, will of God." ROM 12:2 (KJV)

"For which cause we faint not; but though our outward man perish, yet the inward man is renewed day by day." 2 COR 4:16 (KJV)

"And have put on the new man, which is renewed in knowledge after the image of him that created him." COL 3:10 (KJV)

I couldn't understand how the things that once helped me sometimes seemed to turn on me. It appeared that retakes were a common thread for me, and no matter how much I attempted to do my best, I felt like my best was not good enough. The ministry that built me up also became a place that the enemy was using to tear me down.

It was a fight to overcome manipulation and control. The word was used as a hammer for me and a feather for others. Although I was a faithful church member, I found myself being rebuked for little petty things.

There were times I questioned why I was feeling depleted, dishonored, exposed, and isolated. For over ten years, my leader told me that I needed to be in ministry school and training. I went year after year, module after module, and class after class and was rarely given the freedom to use my training in ministry.

I believed my leader, and I was growing, so I endured and stayed the course. The constant buffeting got me to the point where I no longer required milk alone. I now had developed the ability to chew the meat of the Word.

It was the Word that spoke truth and allowed me to divide the wheat from the tare as I struggled between the words being taught to train and equip me or condemn me. I thought it was the Holy Spirit's role to convict us, right?

I found myself in a place where I needed to separate myself from what was familiar and often left me feeling alone and isolated. I came to a point where I just accepted it was time for me to move forward.

I learned that transition is not always easy and often requires discomfort and another level of pressing. This time, I handled things differently. I was determined to hold complete trust in God and not look to find fulfillment in other individuals, ministries, or leaders. I realized that what was put inside of me was valuable.

I enjoyed a new confidence and assurance based on the Word of the Lord. I saw with my own eyes how the equipping of the saints could come in many ways. Ephesians 4:11-13 being worked out in my life.

"And he gave some, apostles; and some, prophets; and some, evangelists; and some, pastors and teachers; For the perfecting of the saints, for the work of the ministry, for the edifying of the body of Christ: Till we all come in the unity of the faith, and of the knowledge of the Son of God, unto a perfect man, unto the measure of the stature of the fullness of Christ."(KJV)

After leaving the ministry, there were still things I had to process, but I was equipped enough to "go and continue to grow". I can now comprehend how my whole life has been under a Divine operation in making me stronger and more confident in God. I am no longer the little girl running from the taunting crowd or full of voids because of who or what was missing from my life. The one who saved me also filled me and brought healing to the wounded places. I am still a work in progress, but I am further along than where I began. My "here" is no longer under the cycle of "again" because I am living in the newness of my Creator.

Throughout my life and relationship with God, I evolved into the woman I am today. I would like to share some of what I gained. The main aspect that I was able to gain throughout this process was a greater level of CONFIDENCE. In the middle of my tears, when I had cried until my eyes were puffy and snot ran down my pillowcases, I had to learn how to praise in the bad times by rehearsing the good times.

Being able to remember how God brought me through the last almost-fainting ordeal gave me enough strength to get a moan upon my lips. Before I knew it, I was singing a song out of my mouth and my joy was returning. Just like Jacob who wrestled with the angel of God until daybreak, I was determined that I would not let go unless God blessed me.

When I let go of trying to be in control, I was able through God to gain control of my fleeting thoughts and defeat the strongholds over my mind. It was in this welcoming place where my confidence was being heighten to new levels. I knew that Jesus was with me and that He had wrapped His arms around me. This was my new safe place. It created the leverage I needed to declare with confidence that I was no longer broken and His power was healing my heart. In His presence, new strategies were being given. What I heard, I would jot down in my journal. Sometimes, these instructions would include who I needed to forgive. These hot-off-the-press Words allowed me to trust more in the God inside of me than the world outside of me. In this process,

God required fasting, praying, and seeking Him like my life depended on it.

These tools empowered me to deal with the fleeting thoughts that often tried to distract me from remaining stable and fixed on the promise of God. The Word that I was applying to my everyday walk allowed me to sit at the feet of seasoned leadership without complaining or regretting. I learned to surrender more of me to gain more of God. I placed a demand on the Holy Spirit within me and He comforted, guided, and kept me.

God was instructing me to cut the strings of dead weight so that I could soar. This meant that I had to disconnect from people who had a negative hold on my emotions, heart, and gift. I had to filter my desire to serve whomever and whenever through the Holy Spirit to ensure I was in balance.

I can look over the distance and see the growth, but I must be vigilant and stay on guard. The enemy still tries to creep around like a lion attempting to separate me from the everlasting LOVE of GOD, but I will not give up on GOD. I stay watchful just as the Word instructs with a cool head so the enemy doesn't catch me napping.

"Keep a cool head. Stay alert. The devil is poised to pounce, and would like nothing better than to catch you napping." 1 Peter 5:8 (MSG)

My progress wasn't easy. Sometimes it was an ugly, grueling process. GOD hid and covered me as He stripped me. It was a private affair. He instructed me on how to create healthy spiritual boundaries and how to distinguish His voice from man's. Being obedient and committing to His process caused the shackle to fall from my ankles and sin and weights to fall from my life so that I could run the race set before me. I am now at a place where I desire to bleed integrity to HIM. I want to speak truly, be truly, and live truly. This requires me to be true to myself first.

I reached a place of contentment when my "YES" unto the Lord became first priority. When fulfilling the destiny of God becomes your "sold out" desire, you will be able to see the big picture.

The afflicting of my soul aligned me with the will of the Father. The price paid to be more like Christ and to be proven faithful to My FATHER is worth more than I can say. The lonely road of sacrifice, although narrow, became a path of delight and happiness because now I can help others who encounter the DELIVERED ME. I now realize everything was to teach me, and even when lessons would make me feel lonely, I was never alone because God has always been there!

"teaching them to observe all that I commanded you; and lo, I am with you always, even to the end of the age." Matthew 28:20

POINTS TO PONDER

1. **"I didn't feel like I belong"**   In life, there will be some lonely days, some dark nights and plenty of injustices, but stay the course. Even when you don't feel like you belong or are wanted, God has moments and encounters to prove His WORD.

2. **"Don't do IT"**
It is simply not enough just to say that phrase. Be ready to teach and explain from the delivered you, because you could be molding someone's future. Being relatable, having compassion, and being Holy Ghost

filled could be the saving grace to a soul that you speak into. Remove the form and get the power.

POINTS TO PRACTICE

1.Don't silence your voice, when you're hurting. Write it out or talk it out, but make sure that you effectively let it out. Release it!

2.   Speak words of affirmation to build yourself up during the stripping process. Put the WORD on it, continuously.

3.   Believe the process enough to stick with it, don't just memorize for the moment but learn it for life. Build a framework that you can work with.

POINTS TO PRAY

1.Pray first! Talking about a matter without praying about it is all in vain. If you want a true solution to the matter, you must pray.

2.   Pray for eyes to see. Whatever captures your attention can potentially make you or break you. The matters of the heart start with what we see, think on, and experience.

3.   Pray for Power. Lights without power will keep you in the dark. Being in the dark blinds you to what lies ahead. Power not only reveals, it removes.

PRAYER

LORD as I move through Your spiritual maturity, keep me by Your Grace and mercy. Let no evil befall me as You hide me from the terror from night. Let my sight be saturated by the vision of You and Your promise.

I pray that my feet move quickly from the pitfalls of life and that my steps be ordered by You to victory. Be a light unto my path and a tour guide on my journey to success. Let my words be after your counsel and guidance. Add learning to my lips and teach my mouth how to talk. Reveal all distractions, disguisers of truth, and naysayers.

I speak peace that passeth all understanding over my being. I call forth help in the time of need and available resources for the cause. For You are My present help, and there is truly none like you. I thank You for Your wise stewards that will pour vast knowledge from their well-spent lives with you. Let the words of my mouth be a testimony of your promise as I declare truth to mankind. In Jesus' Name, Amen.

ABOUT THE AUTHORS

IDELLA LISELLE

People often refer to Idella Liselle as radical and out of the box. Her encounters with the LORD are so real and tangible that any other way of living is simply not an option.

She entered into ministry at a young age with a desire to impact her community from the age of 12 until she graduated Valedictorian at the age of 16. This desire for community development continues to spur her outreach efforts.

She promotes sexual integrity as a viable option. She freely shares her testimony of being delivered from sexual perversion and how she is a virgin to this day. She wanted to ensure that, unlike what was available to her, when people want to be free from sexual perversion, they have a place to go. She has spoken on many platforms against sexual perversion and the pursuit of holiness.

With over 25 years of walking in the prophetic and 20 years of ministry experience, GOD called Idella to pastor. On October

29, 2012, Pastor Idella heard GOD audibly calling her to the role of Apostle.

Since 2009, she has trained countless people on how to hear and recognize GOD's Voice. Idella has a no-nonsense approach to hearing from GOD. She is adamant about keeping it simple. Idella brings further clarity to the prophetic, saying, "not every Christian is a prophet but every Christian can prophesy". Under R.E.A.L. Ministries Institute, she equips men and women of GOD with tools for ministry and/or ordination.

She serves as Lead Pastor of REAL Ministries in Covington, GA and is the CEO of several enterprising endeavours including Idella Liselle Consulting & Management and Kingdom BAD Girls.

Contact Information
idellaliselle@gmail.com
www.realministries.rocks
www.idellalliselle.com
www.kingdombadgirls.com
www.publishher.org
FB Info: IdellaLiselle
770-727-1669

JHAKI DAVIS

Jacqulyn A. Jarmon-Davis, affectionately called **Jhaki**, has profound passion in serving GOD and His people. The youngest of her siblings, grew up in a musical Christian-military household, which afforded opportunities to travel to different places and meet diverse people. While meeting others, it was through the love of communication which contributed to Jhaki's desire to teach and train others. Eventually, that passion added in helping others to discover their life's purpose while maximizing their GOD given potential and to live authentically, while serving in this present age.

Upon graduating from high school, Jhaki attended Gulf Coast Community College, then received her license through Bert Rodgers Real Estate School and in 2012, graduated *summa cum laude* from *In Christ International Bible College* and presently attending Dayspring Theological Seminary.

Presently a member and serves as Psalmist, musician and Minister of Music. Jhaki is also on the ministerial staff and board of elders of the Love Center Church, Inc. and Love Center Ministries Worldwide, Inc. In the professional arena, Jhaki is a domestic violence counselor and volunteer chaplain for incarcerated females.

Through JD Music Ministries, for which Jhaki is founder and CEO, she has worked closely with several singing groups and individuals on their musical projects. GOD has opened numerous doors of opportunities through this musical venue. Along with two other young ladies, a single entitled, *"Thank You for Your Mercy"* was released. Recently, her long awaited project, a book, "Walls Do Talk" is in circulation. Other publications include, The Love Center Cookbook and Music Ministry Digest, Vol. I.

Along with her husband, Bishop Robert L. Davis and their son, R. Damien J. Davis, they serve in ministry together and are residents in Florida.

"Life Is the Song: Love Is the Music"

Contact Information:
jdmusicministry@aol.com
jhakidavis3160@gmail.com

Facebook Info:
Jhaki Davis

LISA JOHNSON

Lisa Johnson is a native of Richmond, VA, and she started this journey of dance in 1996. Her gift of dance has propelled her to travel all over the world, including the Bahamas, Brazil, and the Philippines. She uses her dance as warfare against the enemy and as worship and intimacy with God.

Dance and flagging is a language that all can understand, and when meshed with the presence of God, true transformation can take place. God continues to stretch Lisa to new levels of excellence as she encourages and deposits a true passion and dedication to God in worship and intercession.

In the beginning of her journey, Lisa did not have a healthy self-worth, confidence, or strength. She struggled with rejection, offense, and her need for love, which resulted in her looking in all the wrong places.

Since this time, Lisa has grown and matured into a true woman of God and a prophetic worshipper. Her journey had its difficulties, defeat, and warfare, but she is still standing through it all because of God! She has truly discovered for herself that greater is He within her than he who is in the world. Know there is power in the Blood of Jesus! He will never leave you nor forsake you. When you are real with God, He will be real with you - no sugar coating, just truth! Ask God to help you find the "illusions," deceptions, & lies in your life and shine His light on them for His truth to be revealed.

Remember, only when truth is fully embraced can it truly set you free. He who is free is free indeed!

For speaking engagements or contact, use the information below.
Contact Information:
Flagdancer7@gmail.com

JULIE JONES

Julie Jones loves to share the gift of joy with all those she encounters. There is so much that goes on around us, and it is the joy of the LORD that gives us strength and the fuel to endure. HE gives you beauty for ashes. Many of us grow up not knowing our true value and worth.

Knowing your identity in Christ Jesus positions you for all that HE wills for you, a future and a hope. Allow HIM to turn detours and dead ends into the destiny HE longs for you to walk in!

Julie resides in upstate New York with her 3 daughters, Destiny, Cera, and Cloe.

Her passion is for all to know and believe that we are fearfully and wonderfully made from the inside out. HE is the master designer, and we are adorned in HIS image and likeness for HIS glory. It's the adorning of our hearts that cause us to shine like a precious gem.

Do not let your adorning be external—the braiding of hair and the putting on of gold jewelry, or the clothing you wear— but let your adorning be the hidden person of the heart with the imperishable beauty of a gentle and quiet spirit, which in God's sight is very precious. 1 Peter 3:3-4

Contact Information:
Discoveringjewelz@gmail.com

TAMIKU THOMPSON

Evangelist Tamiku Thompson was born in Mississippi, and in 1990, she joined the U.S. Army and travelled internationally and nationally until 1998.

Evangelist Thompson received Jesus Christ at a very young age, and it was evident that she was set apart, for she would spend devoted time kneeling on her knees and singing hymns alongside the mothers of the church.

Evangelist Thompson entered the Prophetic and Ministerial Training Academy in 1992. She is licensed as a Registered Nurse and has served with passion in this field since 1999.

This passion to serve people is evident by her commitment and continual devotion to God's will for her life and the life of others she serves daily.

She has a women's ministry called "Who Can Find Her" that was birthed from her own life story and spiritual womb in 2013. She has a passion for people, but especially the singles, and her ambition is to see them saved, healed, delivered, and whole.

Evangelist Thompson is currently residing in Atlanta, Ga. If you would like to have her as a guest speaker, please contact her using information below.

Contact Information:
tamikut@yahoo.com.

ELIZABETH RIVERA WEBB

Elizabeth Webb is a native of New York who has always loved music and singing. In 1997, she received a Bachelor of Arts Degree as a graduate from Grace Christian College.

In 2007, she was ordained as the Minister of Music at Destiny City Fellowship where she has developed a team of worshippers to serve in the house of the Lord. In October 2017, she was ordained as Pastor over the worship team of Lux Church.

Elizabeth moves in the prophetic song and teaching. She is a speaker encouraging the body of Christ to pursue God's presence and to grow in their gifts. Elizabeth has a passion to lead people into the presence of God and see worshippers developed in the house of the Lord. She teaches worship workshops and leads groups to build the body of Christ.

Elizabeth is currently residing in Richmond, VA /with her husband, Richard Webb. If you would like to have Elizabeth as a guest speaker, please contact her using the information below.

Contact Information:
Liz.rivera7@gmail.com

Is Church Killing You?

Surviving Ministry

Idella McIntyre

Foreword by Pastor Riva Tims

Is Church Killing You?
Surviving Ministry Book Excerpt

Deception can only be effectively played on the stage of life if you have the leading role.

The Art of Deception

> *"And He said, Go and tell this people, Hear ye indeed but understand not; and see ye indeed, but perceive not. Make the heart of this people fat, and make their ears heavy, and shut their eyes; lest they see with their eyes; lest they hear with their ears, and understand with their heart and convert and be healed."* **Isaiah 6:9-10(KJV)**

Whenever you identify church hurt there is a connecting thread of deception. In my experience with church hurt, I saw deception of man which opened my eyes to the other deception around me and an even greater deception within me.

My encounter with deception brought amazing discoveries. I was determined to never be deceived again. I even purchased a book called, *Never Be Lied to Again*. I was challenged to know what was real from what was Memorex. What was the church that GOD wanted me to experience, and what was the church that I had created through opinions and excuses of man?

I was being inducted into a church that allowed people to lead with no consequences to sin, error, or accountability. I was a faithful member to the church of humanity. It sounds strange when announced like that, but are you a member?

97

This church stands with the statement of faith that we are only human. This excuses the accountability that comes with Christian living and leadership within the Body of CHRIST. I am not denying the frailties that lie within each and every one of us, but when did it become okay to answer sin with excuses that tout a don't-judge-me message?

Where are the screams of a brokenness that acknowledge, "I was wrong and I want to be restored"? Where is the restored leadership that becomes transparent with a determination that will bear all so that the trap and proclivities that claim hundreds and even thousands at their sin have a voice crying in the wilderness that there is a better way?

Deception is strong and strategic to the church hurt festering in the Body of CHRIST. Often, the fact is, no one wants to deal with the reality of our conditions, and because of the implications of truth, they choose to rest in the comfort of being deceived.

If I claim I don't see it, then what responsibility do I have to deal with it? According to the Macmillan Dictionary, deception is defined as the act of deceiving or being deceived. Deception is a dual poison. It cannot be given without being received. Deception is a tool that is often implemented by the devil with the ultimate purpose to stop the conversion and healing of a person. The enemy understands that if he can lock us up in lies, we will never be set free. **John 8:32 (KJV)** states, *"And you shall know the Truth and the Truth will set you free."*

In intercession for the Body of CHRIST, GOD challenged me to pray against deception. This question of deception plagued me and caused me to seek GOD for greater understanding. The question that challenged me was how one gets entangled in deception. I use the word, "entangled," because deception is like a web that locks us into a position and stops our spiritual momentum.

As I was looking outward to find my answers, an inner tug told me that my search need not go too far. During a session in prayer, GOD showed me a vision of a wash bucket with spiders floating on the top. I immediately understood the revelation but simultaneously assumed that this was for someone else. I boasted to my mom that GOD was washing someone of deception. I did so with the mention of someone else's name and she then challenged me with the question, "Could it be you that GOD is washing of deception?"

Immediate defense entered. "Not me!" I thought, "I am righteous. I fast and pray. I seek GOD continually." My defense was an alarm that help was needed.

I earnestly sought GOD to understand what He was saying. On first approach to this subject, I could readily see how other mighty men and women of GOD were deceived by looking at them. Their many actions and continuing erroneous stand told me that we could not be reading and understanding the same Scriptures. I could easily point fingers and stand on my righteous soap box, yell until the cows came home, and rant about the deceit and treachery that I witnessed at the hands of those who claimed titles of the most spiritual elite. Yet it was my own heart that had grown fat.

Order Your Book Today

www.publishher.org or **www.realministries.rocks**

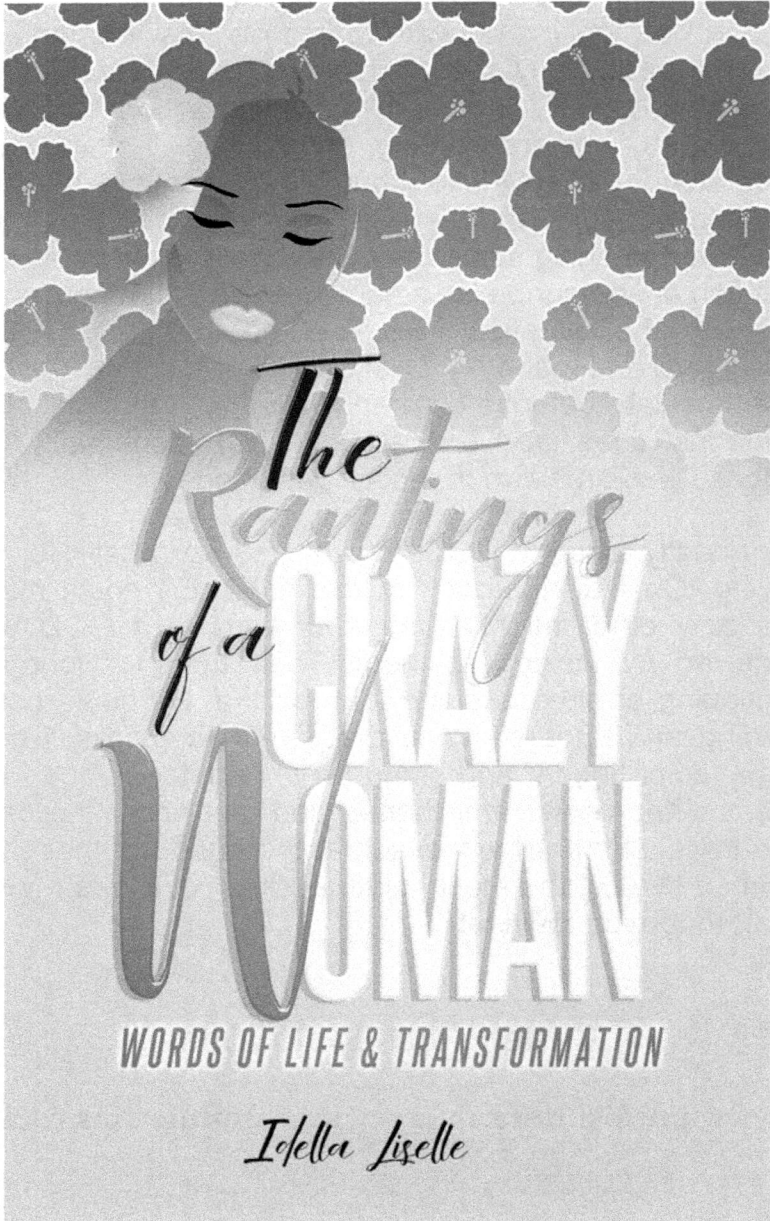

The Rantings of a CRAZY WOMAN

WORDS OF LIFE & TRANSFORMATION

Idella Liselle

Rantings Of A Crazy Woman
Book Exerpt

WELCOME TO MY WORLD

Welcome to my world - one that is consistently crazy! During the compilation of these stories, I was in an interesting place. I was going to church with a smile on my face but coming home thinking that there has got to be more than this. Don't get me wrong. My ministry was taking off, but it still felt like a walk that should have been a run. People looking on the outside thought that my life was peaches and cream, which is fine for some, but GOD promised me strawberry shortcake. I was very aware that this is not it! Through that time, I started getting distracted.

This distraction was deadly. It consumed my focus and retarded my stride. It could have been catastrophic if left unchecked. It was the dark shadow that clouded my sunny days, constantly lurking around, demanding my attention.

This distraction was not a man. My distraction was called lack spiritual lack, emotional lack, physical lack, financial lack, and relational lack. I allowed it to announce itself on every level. As I looked at the vision that I was to run and how ill equipped I was, I began to panic. My panic led to frustration and then inner turmoil. I was looking at the picture of my destiny, trying to decipher the many colors. The colors started bleeding and blending to the point I did not know where one color stopped and another began. It was tiring.

No one knew. Being saved for a considerable amount of time allows for some very skilled performances. We know what to say and how to act. I had it down pat. I can minister to you and you never know that I am hurting. I found it hard to trust others to handle my pain, so I masked it beyond excellent service. Mind you, the service isn't fake; it is genuine, but hollow.

I found it easy to believe the LORD for others. For others, I can tear down walls and leap over troops. I will fight for them. But very seldom did I find it easy to fight for me. I would put my needs on the back burner until I smelled smoke. What was in the pot to serve a hungry people became inedible. Reverently afraid of making someone sick because of ill prepared food, I stopped cooking my own food and just assisted others with their meal.

It is easy to hide behind the crowd. But when GOD is calling one to lead, the need for obedience becomes crucial because the reality is, someone is waiting for your obedience.

CRAZY ON PURPOSE: SEEING WHAT OTHERS CAN'T SEE

CRAZY ON PURPOSE

SEEING WHAT OTHERS CAN'T SEE

IDELLA LISELLE

CRAZY ON PURPOSE

Book Excerpt

"Idella, they are not going to pick you. You don't look like what they want." Those words rang out from a conversation with my mother about an opportunity to sing on a praise team of a megachurch I was attending. It was true that I didn't look like the rest of them. My big afro, ripped clothes or alternating head wraps didn't look like anyone on the stage. But I didn't care. I told myself, NO ONE was going to tell me how to act or what to wear again. I lied.

In my experience, church had done a number on me. Wear this, do that. The commands were continuous. I received instruction without insight and the inward rebellion started. I was adamant that I was going to be different. This time, I was determined that I wasn't going to fit their mold.

The goal had the enemy laughing at me from behind. His plans were at work. My bravado to be different was filled with undercurrents of insecurities. What looked like a strong stand of singularity was a misguided ruse used to separate and alienate me from others and distract me from my purpose.

I knew I was different but didn't know why I was different. Man's tradition had beat me down. Legalistic doctrine hindered my balanced understanding of my uniqueness and its objective. I was taught that in order to be a leader, I had to look a certain way and carry myself a certain way. In principle I agree, my challenge came into play when the persona I was to emulate wasn't GOD's but man's tradition making His word of no effect. When we place a greater importance on clothes than character, "Houston we have a problem".

I wanted to fight back, but my arsenal was carnal. I hadn't taken the time to get a true battle plan. Any fight determined to effectively win, is to first deal with strongholds. My thoughts weren't targeted. My passion caused a public revolt that appeared contrary to those watching because of the lack of revelation. I was intentionally pushing people out of their comfort zones in how I dressed or what I said.
I was ready to prove anyone wrong who limited GOD's power to a long skirt and a covered head. In many of my circles bright colored hair didn't fit into the mold of what an anointed woman of GOD looked like, so one color wasn't enough, I needed multiple colors.

I was at odds with what I loved. I loved church, yet, hated how church wanted us all to look the same and sound the same. I hated the uniforms we had to wear. ALL wear white, ALL wear black and even gave orders how it was to be worn. I couldn't understand how uniformity constituted as unity. We could all have the same things on and still be disjointed and disconnected.

As time progressed, I continually tried to buck the system that I had once fully participated in. I recall the wasted dollars on trying to look the part. In some settings, the look I had to produce was two-piece suits, with sequined collars and big church hats. When I was laid off the job that allowed my continuous purchases of the church look, I discovered a truth. I DON'T LIKE MATCHY - MATCHY SUITS OR CHURCH HATS. I actually like separates and look better in them.

Let's get this straight. Clothes weren't the problem; they were only a symptom. Clothes within itself are not the issue. I don't think there is anything wrong with those who like long skirts, big hats and sequined church suits. If you like it, I love it. However, I didn't like those things, even as a teenager, I felt the austerity of some clothes were bondage to me. However, being told that wearing these types of clothes was what I needed to lead and become who man approved of; I denied my uniqueness. Have you ever done that?

The fact that so many diverse women will be reading this book, I believe that I do need to set some parameters. If you being you causes one to connect with sin, it ain't GOD. GOD did not free us so that we could wear skirts and dresses so tight that people can see our breath before it comes out. Nor so short that they see our behinds or shirts that reveal an inordinate amount of cleavage. Again, clothes aren't the problem but a symptom. When we are okay with our clothes being the greatest representation of who we are, there is a deeper issue at play.

Because I felt that my identity was connected to what I wore, I took it personal. Whenever you make a fight personal you lose out on the power of purpose. I recognize that because I serve a GOD of purpose, everything that happens to me is for purpose.

Purpose identifies, ignites and instructs us. Purpose is our true definition of meaning. Some people wait a lifetime to find purpose while others appear to have known theirs from birth. I came into mine in increments. The more I discovered who GOD is, the more I discovered more of who I was. My purpose started to resemble a glaringly loud alarm that demanded I wake up. It was time I did something!

ORDER YOUR BOOK TODAY!!
www.publishher.org

Are you an Aspiring Author

Do you have a story to tell? Are you a Kingdom BAD Girl? Would youlike to be an author in our next compilation or have a book you need assistance in publishing? For more information go to **www.publishher.org**

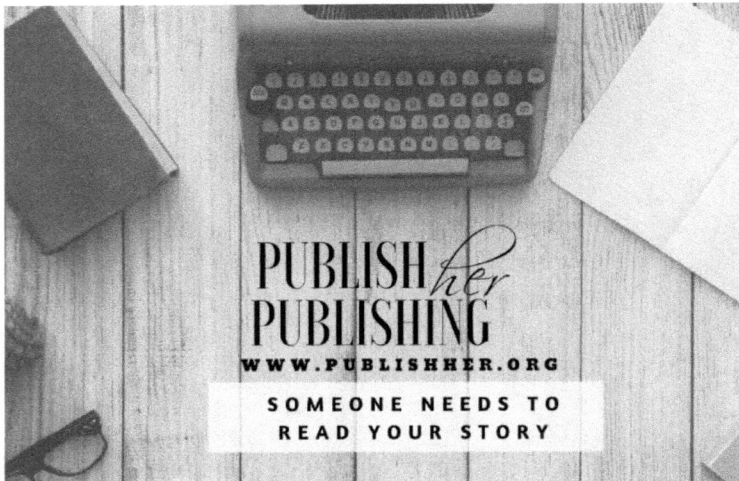

What is a Compilation?

Compilation books are written by more than 1 Author on a subject. Each author submits their contribution based on the subject matter. These submissions comprise one book. Compilation books present authors with a great opportunity for book publishing and increased self- promotion.

Reasons Why Authors Should Consider Book Compilation Publishing

Cheaper way to get your writings into print: Book publishing can be very expensive. Many facets have to be taken into consideration that could affect the price of publishing a complete manuscript. The number of pages, the size of the book and colored images can change the price drastically. When you connect with other Authors, you lessen the cost quite considerably.

Product Development. Products are a necessary component for success. New products and services are the lifeblood of any business. Ministry is also a service industry with little choice but grow and improve if they want to move from surviving to thriving. The new products and services created provide the mechanism for this growth and improvement.

Promotions. This opportunity allows you to become unforgettable. You can get your website and book name in front of a whole new audience by being in a compilation book. (If you need a website, please consult our PublishHer team for some amazing packages.)

You can make a nice profit: As one of the authors, you are able to buy additional copies of the book at a very low cost and sell it at a retail price which can increase your income.

Other people promote you. Each of the authors will place you in front of a new audience. As people read their book, they come across you and connect to you and your purpose.

Low Minimums. You can order copies of the compilation 24 hours, 7 days a week with as little at 10 at a time. Only those who have Authored the compilation will be allowed to purchase at the special Comp price.

Leverage. By presenting yourself with other notable authors, you increase your credibility

Purpose. Last but definitely not least, this opportunity positions you to fulfill your purpose and WRITE A BOOK.

If you have any questions, contact us 678-744-4KBG or email publishherpublishing@gmail.com

Are You Ready To Take This Trip on the ROAD?

Globe Trotters
Empowering Women All Around The World

MISSIONS EVERY
r
DECEMBER

For more info email KingdomBADGirls@gmail.com

Are you mission minded? You want to travel the world making an impact and having fun. Join us every December as we travel outside our comfort zones to empower people and offer a holistic approach at successful living.

LEARN HOW TO LEAD FROM THE INSIDE OUT

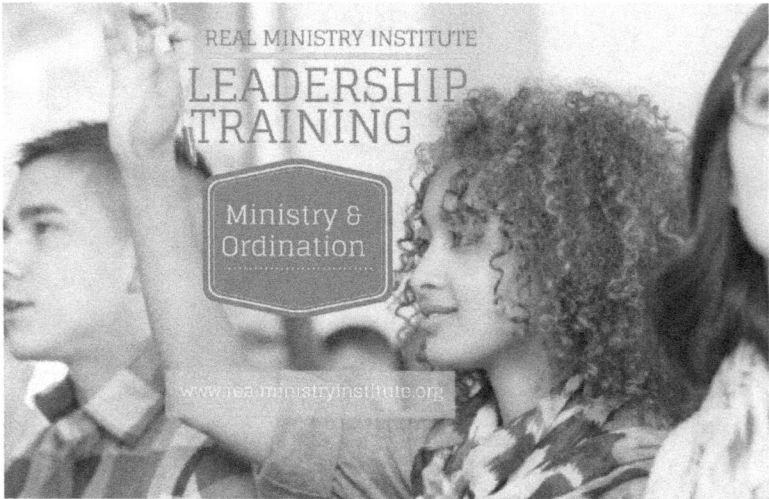

ARE YOU CALLED TO MINISTRY? Want to be trained to lead from the inside out? Would an environment that could cultivate the gift on the inside be worth an investment? If so, go to **www.realministryinstitute.org** for more information.

**SHE WASN'T LOOKING FOR A PRINCE.
SHE WAS LOOKING FOR A SWORD**

A Program For Empowerment
For Ages 15-21

For more information
WWW.KINGDOMBADGIRLS.COM